Jacob A.

Riis

Photographer
& Citizen

The Last Portrait of Jacob A. Riis
(Probably 1912–1913)

Jacob A. Riis

Photographer & Citizen

by
Alexander Alland, Sr.
with Preface by Ansel Adams

An Aperture Book

Aperture, Inc., publishes a Quarterly of Photography, portfolios, and books to communicate with serious photographers and creative people everywhere. A catalog of publications is available upon request.

Published in the United States by Aperture, Inc., Elm Street, Millerton, New York 12546, and simultaneously in Canada by Gage Trade Publishing, Agincourt, Ontario, and in Great Britain by Gordon Fraser Gallery Limited, London, England.

Library of Congress Catalog Card Number 74-21617
ISBN 0-912334-66-5

Manufactured in the United States of America.
The design is by David Epstein.

Printed by Falcon Press, and bound by Sendor Bindery.

9 8 7 6 5 4 3 2
First Printing

For: Alexandra,
Alexander Jr., and Sonia,
David and Julie

Dear Alexander Alland:

. . . Had it not been for your unself-seeking work, the negatives would still be where they were, in oblivion.

—Roger William Riis

South Kent, Conn., Dec. 7, 1948

Contents

Introduction

Beginning in 1888 with a camera he scarcely knew how to use, Jacob Riis established a great tradition in American photography. He took pictures to document and expose the everyday misery of the despairing and often unseen poor. During the ten years that he made photographs, no one—not even Riis—thought of Jacob Riis as a photographer. Now, since the rediscovery of his dramatic pictures in 1946, it is often forgotten that he was an outstanding journalist, writer and lecturer — one of the first of the great reformers who came to be known as muckrakers.

In this study of Riis as citizen and photographer I have attempted to compact the long and versatile career of a remarkable man and show how his many roles converged in a crusade for human decency. His book *How the Other Half Lives,* published in 1890, was both the first exposé to be illustrated with documentary photographs and a landmark in the battle for social justice. Soon after its publication he became a nationally acclaimed writer and lecturer. His lectures carried unprecedented immediacy and impact because they were illustrated with lantern slides made from his revealing photographs.

Before me as I write is a circular from a national organization dated December 1973: a plea for moral and financial support to ease the suffering of the poor, it says in part, "the despair that lives behind crumbling tenement walls is unbelievable to those who have never experienced it." Nearly a century before, Jacob Riis not only experienced the slums of New York City but submerged himself with pen and camera in the same continuing struggle against human misery. He wrote, "The sights I saw there gripped my heart until I felt that I must tell of them or burst."

The eighty-two illustrations in this book are reproduced from the carefully controlled enlarged prints that I made from the original 4 × 5 glass negatives when the Jacob A. Riis Collection was reposited in the Museum of the City of New York.

The greatest reward in having a book published is that it provides an opportunity to publicly acknowledge the generous help given to the author. I should like to thank Grace Mayer who for thirty years shared my interest in Riis and bore with my zeal in promoting him; Ansel Adams for his penetrating and deeply moving assessment of Riis as a photographer and citizen; Dr. J. Riis Owre for his kind patience in answering my endless queries about his grandfather; Beaumont and Nancy Newhall for their friendly reponse in sharing their expertise with me; Felix J. Cuervo for his unflagging efforts to keep alive the name of Jacob Riis; Ronald Bailey for his perceptive editorial advice and assistance. Also to many others whom I involved in my project–especially Betty Foster, Albert K. Baragwanath and Mogens Bencard. I am grateful to the Macmillan Publishing Company for granting me permission to quote from the Epilogue to their 1970 re-publication of *The Making of an American.*

Alexander Alland, Sr.
North Salem, New York, 1974

Preface

To my list of intense experiences in photography, including a preview of some Strand negatives in Taos, the Portraits and Shells of Weston, the Equivalents of Stieglitz and the magnificent human affirmation of Dorothea Lange, I must add the Riis-Alland prints displayed at the Museum of the City of New York.

For me these are magnificent achievements in the field of humanistic photography . . . I know of no contemporary work of this general character which gives such an impression of competence, integrity and intensity.

I find it difficult to explain my convictions. I am not thinking of Riis's achievement in terms of comparative equipment and materials (that is a line worn thin by now). Obviously, Alland's beautiful prints, by exalting the physical qualities of Riis's work, intensify their expressive content. The factual and dated content of subject has definite historic importance, but the larger content lies in Riis's expression of people in misery, want and squalor. These people live again for you in the print — as intensely as when their images were captured on the old dry plates of ninety years ago. Their comrades in poverty and suppression live here today, in this city — in all the cities of the world. I have thought much about this intense, *living* quality in Riis's work; I think I have an explanation of its compelling power. It is because in viewing those prints I find myself identified with the people photographed. I am walking in their alleys, standing in their rooms and sheds and workshops, looking in and out of their windows. And they in turn seem to be aware of me.

In so much photography of people in our time I feel that the photographer is cloaked in invisibility; he captures a fragment of the world without identifying himself with his immediate environment. Perhaps he thinks he achieves identification — but only the spectator of his photograph can be sure. He seems to avoid detection; no one in his pictures seems to recognize him or acknowledge his presence. It is a peephole — or keyhole — view point: the sly capturing of the private moment, the time-slice of turmoil, the "observation" of the little man who wasn't there!

I remember a photographic educator who violently condemned any picture in which the subject "mugged" the camera. His concept of a picture was suspiciously reminiscent of an aquarium thronged with weary, uninterested fish, or a stage of posturing puppets. I fortified myself by recalling Strand's wonderful Mexican photographs; in many of these the subjects are looking at you — you are there with them, you may almost speak to them. Because of this intimacy, reality is magically intensified, another dimension of response is added to the dimensions of statement. Do I hear the word "empathy"?

Many of the people shown in Riis's work looked at the camera and the photographer at the moment of exposure. They did not realize that they were looking at you and me and all humanity for ages of time. Their postures and groupings are not contrived; the moment of exposure was selected more for the intention of truth than for the intention of effect.

It would be difficult to imagine these photographs as single images apart from the great matrix of Riis's project. Riis's photographs, books, articles and lectures exist as a *unit statement*, a consuming lifework. This is what photography should be — an integrated creative and constructive statement, not a series of disconnected and unorganized images of more or less superficial appeal. The photographer when "expressing himself" or reflecting an ideological or purely aesthetic line is, in effect, shadowboxing with reality. The larger aspects of reality — humanity, nature in implied or direct relation to humanity — cannot be compressed into stylized, intellectual patterns. Statements which are built upon and express truthful intention will seldom be ineffective. The mechanics of communication partake of truth when truth is the objective. The techniques of the pictorialist and the esoteric abstractionist often reflect the weakness of their concept and expression. In Riis's work I am never conscious of technique, methods or means — only of appropriate and efficient mechanical necessities. As revealed in the Alland prints, the quality of his flash illumination is extraordinary; the plastic shadow-edges, modulations and textures of flesh, the balance of interior flash and exterior daylight — what contemporary work really exceeds it in competence and integrity?

Ansel Adams

7

Jacob A. Riis: *Photographer & Citizen*

. . . Faint with hunger, I sat down on the steps under
illuminated clock, while Bob stretched himself at my feet.
He had beguiled the cook in one of the last houses
we called at, and his stomach was filled. From the corner
I had looked enviously. For me there was no supper,
as there had been no dinner and no breakfast. To-morrow there
was another day of starvation. How long was this to last?
Was it any use to keep up a struggle so hopeless?

—*The Making of an American*

Chapter 1

"The Mightiest Lever"

Two unique attributes of photography attracted Jacob Riis and enabled him to become — nearing forty and a reporter by trade — America's first true journalist-photographer. First, the camera is unsurpassed for recording what is there; words describe, the camera shows. Second, formal training is not a necessity; even with the primitive equipment of Riis's day, a neophyte could become a proficient photographer in a relatively short time. What mattered, then as now, was the use one made of the camera. To some early photographers it was a toy for passing the time, to others an instrument for expressing artistic sensibility. To a humanist like Riis it was a weapon, to be taken up as he had taken up the pen, to battle for social justice. "The power of fact is the mightiest lever of this or of any day," he wrote in his autobiography *The Making of an American.* He saw in the photograph a supreme weapon of fact, a mighty lever for exposing, persuading, convicting. A half-century before Henry Luce made publishing history with a magazine devoted to pictures, Riis knew the truth of Luce's assertion: "The photograph is not the newest, but is the most important instrument of journalism which has developed since the printing press."

Riis's extraordinary photographic legacy was accomplished in a short duration. In 1887 he enlisted two amateur photographers and then two professionals to illustrate his stories with pictures made instantaneously by means of a new technique — flash powder. A few months later Riis himself bought a camera outfit and went to Potter's Field to make his first photographs. Only one plate turned out: a dramatically overexposed view of a common grave. Some ten years later, he put away the camera and apparently never again took it up. He had made enough photographs to document his writings and lectures. The collection that survived him is testimony to the extreme practicality with which he approached photography. It embraces 412 glass-plate negatives consisting of original pictures taken by Riis and by four other men, a large number of copy negatives of pictures and drawings Riis obtained from the files of the Society for the Prevention of Cruelty to Children, Rogues Gallery, Board of Health, and the Children's Aid Society, and a few subjects copied from commercially sold stereographs. The negatives by Riis himself probably do not exceed 250, though those he made for his newspaper stories undoubtedly disappeared into the files of the newspaper and were lost. He photographed only what he needed. Moreover, the new flash-powder technique filled the room with such dense smoke that taking more than one exposure often was out of the question. "I came to take up photographing . . . not exactly as a pastime," Riis wrote. "It was never that with me. I had use for it, and beyond that I never went. I'm downright sorry to confess here that I'm no good at all as a photographer."

The marked contrast between Riis's work and that of his better-known contemporary Alfred Stieglitz encapsulates two divergent streams of twentieth-century photography. Stieglitz, who almost single-handedly elevated the status of photography to that of a fine art, used the camera to create; Riis used it to record. One believed that the camera should portray the beauty that nature wrought, the other used it to record the ugliness wrought by man. The work of Stieglitz is photography at its creative best — living facsimiles of nature's images, expanded vistas caught in a mirror. Riis's photographs are not pretty pictures. Sordid documents, they aroused the public indignation that led to many vital reforms. Both men were visionaries, whose photographs today are treasured, studied and often exhibited side by side. Between the two extremes lies the spectrum of human experience and the range of individual preference.

Stieglitz, returning to New York in 1890 after several years abroad, found himself assaulted "almost physically" by the naked squalor of the city's streets. Walking down Broadway one evening, he happened upon the performance of a then unknown actress Eleonora Duse; only the prospect of occasionally seeing something with the quality and beauty of her performance made it possible for him to stay on in America. In that same year Riis published *How the Other Half Lives,* his compassionate account of the people-strewn streets that seemed so stifling to Stieglitz. "The belief that every man's experience ought to be worth something to the community from which he drew it . . . made me begin this book," Riis wrote in his introduction. "The story is dark enough, drawn from the plain public records, to send a chill to any heart. If it shall appear that the sufferings and the sins of the 'other half' and the evil they breed, are but a just punishment upon the community that gave it no other choice, it will be because that is the truth."

Lewis Mumford has written of Stieglitz: "One of the most moving and impressive pictures Stieglitz ever made was that of a little tree in Madison Square Park, young and vernal in the rain, with a street sweeper in the foreground, and the dim shape of a building in the background: the promise of life, its perpetual re-awakening and renewal are in that print. Wherever Stieglitz turns his head in the city he looks for the touch of life."

To me, Riis's most moving picture is that of a little child with waxen skin lost in the emptiness of a dank stair landing. The child has the saddest eyes I have ever seen. In stark drama this photograph matches the paintings of Francisco Goya who, before Riis, had used his pictures to show man's gross immorality and cruelty. Riis described how he took the child's picture: "I went up the dark stairs in one of the tenements and there I trod upon a baby. It is the regular means of introduction to a tenement house baby . . . but I never have been able to get used to it. I went off and got my camera and photographed that baby standing with its back against the public sink in a pool of filth that overflowed on the floor."

Before Riis's day, photography was pretty much the province of a small group of professionals. They took portraits on commission or produced for sale remarkably beautiful, sharp and clear views of faraway places. I remember how, as a boy in my hometown of Sebastopol in the Crimea, I marveled at the pictures taken under fire by the Englishman Roger Fenton in the Valley of the Shadow of Death. He traveled to Crimea during the war in 1855 to become the first combat photographer in history. A few years after him the scenes most in demand were the pyramids of Egypt and the wonders of other little-known lands. In America, of course, Mathew Brady's celebrated photographs of the Civil War were widely collected. Later, grandiose views of the West came into fashion, especially those taken with a stereoscopic camera. Called stereographs, these pictures created lifelike, three-dimensional images when seen through a viewer.

The invention of dry plates and albumin printing paper in the late 1880's simplified photography. By Riis's day it no longer was necessary to transport huge cameras, chemicals and portable darkrooms to the scene. Photography clubs sprang up all over the country and began squabbling about whether photography was a fine art, a science or a craft. Many photographers, striving to be artists, resorted to all kinds of tricks to make their prints look like paintings — throwing the image out of focus, interposing it with screens, using multiple printing and chemical manipulations. The final product, greatly admired then, is still highly prized, costly and scarce.

About the turn of the century, Alfred Stieglitz and a small group of followers repudiated their dependence on such manipulation and began to practice straight photography. They had learned to correlate the visible and hidden factors that control the qualities of a photograph. Stieglitz's vehicle for propounding his new views was the New York Society of Amateur Photographers, which in the 1890's had been so intrigued by the advent of the bicycling era that it considered transforming itself into a bicycle club. Stieglitz saved the society from the beckoning asphalt of Broadway by promising to rebuild the club, organize exhibitions and publish the new *Camera Notes*. His work raised the standards of photography to the point where it ceased to be considered an imitative medium. Actually, Stieglitz and his friends did not invent anything new but went back full-circle to the original intent of Daguerre and Niépce, the inventors of photography, who sixty years before had found a mechanical means for recording images that approximated those seen by the human eye.

After photography was recognized as a fine art, that recognition embraced only pictures for pictures' sake. In the credo of one group, the Pictorial Photographers of America, this meant: "Pictures of beauty, originality and of artistic self expression, as distinguished from mere record photography." (This credo was at least a model of clarity. Other aesthetes fed photo-club members hogwash such as: "The esthetic, selfless, sympathetic touch of man upon his fellows, masculine or feminine, subhuman and inanimate as well as human which it organizes and the sense of life itself, and the intense respect for it in all its forms, and the feeling of its wonders communicated by it, provide a basis for relationships and a commonwealth of responsible, self-regulatory individuals, and democracy. . . .") It was many years before museums overcame their aversion to documentary photography. The simple yet magnetic appeal of Jacob Riis's pictures helped break down the resistance. In 1970 twelve of his prints were included in a group show at the Metropolitan Museum of Art — an event that would have caused a riot forty years earlier.

Even today, some critics question Riis's credentials as a photographer. They are disturbed by the relatively brief duration of his photography and his technical shortcomings. Millions of citizens take pictures today, but are they photographers? My son, an anthropologist, constantly uses still and motion-picture cameras in his work. Countless others make snapshots for pleasure. Riis qualifies as a photographer by at least two definitions: Webster's "one who is engaged in the business of taking pictures" and the more exalted standard laid down almost a century ago by the celebrated spokesman for naturalistic photography, Dr. P. H. Emerson, who said pictures should be judged by "the truth of sentiment and high intellectual standards." The allegation of poor technique is more difficult to rebut. And yet every time I doubt Riis's photography because of its unquestioned technical shortcomings, I recall a story that puts technique in proper perspective. In 1939 that photographer of impeccable technique, Edward Weston, toured the Hollywood storage lots of Metro-Goldwyn-Mayer. "Edward was in seventh heaven," his wife wrote, "he couldn't take a step in any direction without seeing something he had to photograph. When he found a whole street full of stairways leading to nowhere he nearly went mad with delight."

Ultimately, not technique but point of view determines whether the photograph will have lasting value. The photographer chooses what image his camera is to record. The power of the choices Riis made is borne out by the tremendous and enduring appeal of his pictures to large and erudite groups of viewers. Given such choices, technique tends to take care of itself. Riis's photographs are like children's drawings — spontaneous, uninhibited, honest. Like things in nature, the people who are his subjects fall into place by themselves and create a visual harmony that at once makes us aware of their reality and of the truth they project.

13

Riis's passionate social viewpoint sets him apart from photographers who have achieved much greater renown. I remember vividly the first time I ever heard a talk by Edward Steichen, some thirty-five years ago when he was the most sought-after photographer in the advertising field. He told of a conversation with the great dancer Isadora Duncan, who had come to New York from Russia to give a concert. She asked him: "Edward, why are you wasting your time here? Come back with me to Moscow. They will give you there a studio and everything you may ask for, and you'll be free to create meaningful art for the people." Steichen looked at the audience and asked, "Do you know what I told her? I said, No, Isadora, no. My place is here in America. There is plenty of hell to be raised right here!" As far as I know, Steichen was not in the habit of making public comments on any of our social, political or economic problems. In two world wars and in Korea, Steichen was in charge of combat photography. He had seen and had access to millions of photographic records of the devastation, brutality and suffering brought on by war. Compiled in his famous book *Family of Man,* these records would have spelled DEATH in any language and would have warned humanity against another global holocaust. While his book shows that the world has become man's single environment, it reeks of the same familiar sentimentality and blind faith in the continuity of the "status quo."

Jacob Riis's photographs are inseparable from his activities as a journalist, his journalism from his own incomparable standards of citizenship. He was one of the first of the great investigative reporters — the muckrakers — and he brought all his considerable skills as a reporter, author, photographer and lecturer to exposing corrupt politics, inhuman housing and the plight of neglected children. For much of his life, his arena was New York City. Others like Lincoln Steffens and Upton Sinclair attacked corruption and social injustice on a national scale. Muckraking, Steffens once suggested, is as old as the prophets of the Old Testament. About the time

Riis came to America, reporters from *The New York Times* exposed the machinations of the infamous Boss Tweed. His chief assistant in the infamous ring of "Forty Thieves" was Richard Connelly, known as "Slippery Dick"! About the time I came to America the press was pouring out the details of the Teapot Dome Scandal. Today, the heirs of the muckrakers have brought to light Watergate and other colossal abuses of governmental power. Columnist Jack Anderson was asked recently on a television show if he minded being called a muckraker. "Not at all," said Anderson. "Unfortunately, there are too few muckrakers for too many muckmakers."

Riis's immediate heirs in photography were a score of idealistic men and women, many of whom worked on documentary assignments for civic organizations that Riis had founded or supported. But the great boom in documentary photography came when social and economic conditions were again at their visible worst, during the 1930's Depression. Nearly everyone who owned a camera fancied himself a documentary photographer. Young artists and photographers transformed lofts and basements into clubs and galleries where they could show their work and debate endlessly whether it was of social value. Some of their photographs helped the cause of social justice. Like Riis, such photographers found a way — in the words of Roy Stryker, who headed the Farm Security Administration documentary team — to "speak, as eloquently as possible, of the things to be said in the language of pictures [and knew] enough about the subject-matter to find its significance in itself and in relation to its surroundings, its time, and its function." Other pictures were not worth the paper they were printed on. There were more photographs taken of ashcans and garbage heaps, of slums and drunken bums, of broken windows and street urchins, than in the entire previous history of American photography. "There was very little truly constructive imagery," wrote Ansel Adams, "photographs that expressed hope or a positive possibility of solutions to the sad Depression situation. It was this blind devotion to an *approach* which disturbed. 'Social significance' to me had at that time the same semantic integrity as 'law and order' does today."

I remember one instance where overzealousness defeated the best of intentions. An exhibit of photographs on housing, "Roofs for 40 Million," was to be held at Rockefeller Center. The directives to photographers read: "The theme is housing but don't limit yourself to slum horrors. The subject is very broad and can be treated satirically, realistically, imaginatively, optimistically, pessimistically, etc., in terms of causes, results, Utopian dreams. The implications of bad housing can be told in tragic human terms: crime, juvenile delinquency, fire hazards, prostitution, disease, crowded schools, sordid interiors. . . ."

The spirit of social concern fostered by the Depression carried over into the formation of the American Artists Congress, some eight hundred nationally recognized artists, sculptors and photographers who came together to oppose Hitler's theories and to strengthen the ideas of democracy at home. Its credo stated: "Art is one of the forms of social development and consciousness, which is in constant interaction with the other social forms. The character of art at any given time stands in definite relation to the social environment . . . including its political, social, economic and cultural aspects, and is a matter of direct concern to all artists who wish to develop as rational human beings." Riis believed that the ills that beset the other half could be remedied only by the will of society once it knew the truth. I learned the value of exposure when in 1939 I was on a photographic assignment to promote tourism in the Virgin Islands. The housing conditions of the inhabitants were so bad that I decided on my own to document them. The photographs appeared in the New York newspaper *PM* and resulted in a Congressional appropriation for housing in the Virgin Islands. The newspaper's "News of Photography" editor, Ralph Steiner, said of the photographs: "Pictures must have roots which are planted below the superficial level to make people feel and act. Certainly no photographic salon will hang these pictures.

But they have been used in Congress to promote good housing in the Islands."

Out of the documentary explosion of the 1930's emerged the new form of photography known as photojournalism. Newspapers gave vastly more space to photographs; new magazines devoted to journalistic pictures came into being. In the last two decades television, with its immediacy and simultaneous transmission of words, pictures and sound, has become the newest form of photojournalism. But there remain the documentary still photographers who, in newspapers and books, carry on the tradition of Jacob Riis.

Ever since 1947, when Riis's photographs were exhibited for the first time, I heard only one adverse criticism of him and his work. His critic perused a *single* Riis volume and saw pictures which were facsimiles of prints made from copy negatives which in turn were made from poor prints. While conceding Riis's effectiveness as a reformer, the critic said: "There is no denying Riis's humanitarianism and energy, and there is no question that he is one of the most effective reformers this country has ever seen, and that he has a place too, in the history of photography. But frankly I see no way, nor reason to obscure the fact that he's crippled as well as ennobled by his intentions, that his awesome single-mindedness, the source of much that is admirable and honorable in him, has as its flipside a simple-mindedness that lands him as often on his head as his feet. . . ."

Perhaps without realizing it, the critic had pinpointed Riis's greatest strength. Riis was a simple man, though hardly simple-minded. His biographer, Dr. Louise Ware, noted that he cared little for music or the theater and "the niceties of literary taste were beyond him." He was not an artist, not a literary stylist. But his very simplicity as a man permitted a single-minded pursuit of social justice rarely matched in journalism. Humanitarian zeal led him to take up in turn the weapons with which he excelled — pen, camera, his own voice on the lecture platform.

Far more complex is the task of finding the sources of Riis's zeal. Saints are not ordained and social reformers not born: they come to their calling through a chain of experiences, influences, even coincidences. Certainly Riis's early immigrant days in the slums of New York provided him with both firsthand knowledge and powerful motives for his later crusades. Among the many other attempts at accounting for the evangelistic eloquence of his pen and camera, none is more dramatic nor plausible than a story told by Riis himself: "In a Methodist revival . . . I had fallen under the spell of the preacher's fiery eloquence. Brother Simmons was one of the old circuit rider's stock . . . the spirit burned within him; he brought me to the altar quickly, though in my case conversion refused to work the prescribed amount of agony. With the heat of the convert, I decided on the spot to take to preaching, but Brother Simmons would not hear of it. 'No, no, Jacob,' he said, 'not that, we have preachers enough. What the world needs is consecrated pens.'"

When Riis came to realize that his pen was not enough, he took up the camera and consecrated it in his crusade. His writing, he said, "did not make much of an impression — these things rarely do, put in mere words — until my negatives, still dripping from the dark-room, came to reinforce them. From them there was no appeal."

Chapter 2

The Young Immigrant

One day in mid-May 1870, Jacob Augustus Riis boarded a small ship in his native Denmark and left for Glasgow, Scotland. There he changed to the steamer *Iowa* and sailed for America. The voyage took sixteen days on stormy seas. Riis, twenty-one and virtually penniless, rode it out in steerage, the notorious stinkhole deep in the hull where immigrants were packed like cattle. He wrote nothing of the voyage except a description of one incident, which reveals a trace of the diplomacy that later tempered his zeal as a reformer. "The meat served to us became so bad as to offend not only our palates, but also our senses of smell. We got up a demonstration, marching to see the captain in a body. . . . As the spokesman, I presented the case briefly and respectfully, and all would have gone well had not the hot blood of Adler risen at the wrong moment. . . . With a sudden upward jerk he caused that official's nose to disappear in the dish."

I too came to America in steerage, fifty years after Riis, and the same kind of salted beef, black and reeking with saltpeter, was served. I would have starved if not for a good Samaritan traveling in first class. She was a call girl, young and pretty, who had come to my photography studio in Constantinople for a portrait sitting whenever she bought a new hat. She spotted me on the deck below her and every night lowered a little bag of leftovers to me. When we docked in New York, steerage passengers had to wait a day to go ashore because the immigration inspectors were on holiday. First-class passengers did not have to wait; they strolled down the gangplank soon after arrival and were taken ashore by launch, my friend among them.

Riis's ship arrived in New York at daybreak on June 4 and, after a twenty-four-hour delay because of fog, cast her anchor before the U.S. Immigration Station, Castle Garden. "It was a beautiful spring morning," Riis wrote, "and as I looked over the rail at the miles of straight streets . . . my hopes rose high that somewhere in this teeming hive there would be a place for me. . . . The love of change belongs to youth, and I meant to take a hand in things as they came along."

Jacob Riis was born May 3, 1849, in the ancient town of Ribe in southwest Denmark. He was the third in a family of fourteen children and one foster daughter. His father, Niels Edward Riis, taught at a centuries-old preparatory academy. The elder Riis, in addition to being a master of Latin and Greek, was well-versed in history and current affairs. To supplement his modest salary he did occasional part-time editorial work for the town newspaper and served as an interpreter when foreign vessels foundered on the nearby coast. Jacob's mother, Caroline, was a cheerful woman with a gift for recounting stories. By the word of relatives, it was an orderly and most affectionate family.

Young Jake received in his father's school a solid foundation in classical subjects and, like all Scandinavian children, was compelled to acquire a good knowledge of English. He preferred playing outdoors, where he invented games based on his favorite stories of the American frontier by James Fenimore Cooper. His independent streak is foreshadowed in the class journal for 1861, when young Jacob was eleven: "J. Riis showed such unseemly behavior that I found it advisable to dismiss him from the classroom; Riis without pencil; Riis without a pen; Riis has forgotten his book; Riis has neglected a written assignment; Riis inattentive [the last three entries were by his father]; Riis has failed to write his Danish compositions; Riis disobedient...." His foster sister once remarked: "Jake was a good boy — his heart was always warm — but he could be as fire to a powder." When Riis was sixty, he recalled his schooldays in *The Old Town*, a proud history of Ribe where kings once lived interspersed with childhood vignettes. "There were 15 of us in the Latin School. The 13 took the straight and narrow road. They were good and they prospered. Hans and I were the black sheep who perennially disputed the dunce seat.... Now, after a lifetime, what was my surprise to find out that of the whole fifteen whom the king had singled out for decorations were Hans and myself!"

Jacob's father wanted him to prepare for a literary career, but young Jake wasn't interested. He wanted to be a carpenter. In fact, there appears to be little in his boyhood to account for his later career, other than occasional help lent in his father's part-time newspaper job. Many years later a magazine article about Riis found a foreshadowing of the reformer: he had found a rat-infested tenement built over a sewer and waged war against the vermin. Actually, the house in question was Jacob's own home and his battles with the rats earned him the nickname "Jacob the Delver."

After a year's apprenticeship with a local craftsman, Riis moved on to Copenhagen to study with a well-known master builder. His son, Roger William, would later theorize that Riis's passion for reform stemmed from the contrast between sylvan Denmark and the tenement-strewn streets of New York. But the Copenhagen where Riis spent four years had its share of poverty and overcrowding. "Curiously enough," wrote Dr. Louise Ware in her biography, "young Jacob appears not to have been aware of these social conditions, which were almost identical with those that shocked him into action a few years later in New York." Much of the four years in Copenhagen he had his mind on a girl from back home. He had met young Elizabeth—he was fifteen and she

not yet thirteen — when he was helping build her foster father's new factory. Her presence had so overwhelmed him that in quick succession he sliced his shinbone with an adz, chopped off a forefinger with an ax and fell off a roof. Now a full-fledged member of Denmark's Carpenters' Guild, he returned home from Copenhagen to find a job and claim his love. He failed at both. Denmark was in the grip of serious unemployment. Elizabeth's foster father rejected him as a suitor. Jacob had heard there was plenty of work in America, a chance perhaps to get rich quick and become a more desirable suitor for Elizabeth. Years later Riis — who was not above poetic license — embellished their parting: "I kissed her hand and went away, my eyes brimming over with tears, feeling that there was nothing in the world for me anymore and that the further I went from her the better.... So I went out in the world to seek my fortune."

The America Riis came to was in the midst of enormous change. It was booming with industry and corruption as the nation evolved from an agricultural economy and suffered growing pains. Congressmen connived with lobbyists; votes for huge appropriations were bought with cigars, costly dinners and outright bribes. The industrial revolution required infusions of cheap manpower, which was recruited in foreign lands. People were on the move along Europe's paths and roads, on foot and by horse and wagon. First by the hundreds then by the thousands they stole across the borders in the dark of night to fulfill their dream, "On to America!" The new immigrants flocked to New York and other big cities where, along with thousands of ex-slaves up from the South, many found themselves unemployed and living in wretched tenements. (Eventually, the new immigrants would fare better than the ex-slaves. Many years later a young black girl spoke for blacks in a white-dominated society when, in answer to the question of what should be done with Hitler after World War II, she wrote, "Put him in a black skin and let him live the rest of his life in America.")

As soon as Riis stepped off the boat, he began preparing himself for the rigors, real and imagined, of life in the new land. In Denmark his friends had given him a going-away gift of $40 and he had thanked them, saying, "I have not forgotten my religion or the 11th commandment: 'Do not let yourself be overtaken by surprise.'" Riis stopped at the first general store he saw in New York and used half the $40 to purchase a huge Navy revolver. He strapped the revolver to his waist and marched up Broadway ready for the worst. Later he wrote that he was "cut . . . to the heart to find the streets actually paved, with no buffaloes in sight, and not a Red man or a beaver hat." A friendly policeman spotted the revolver and suggested Riis put it away.

After a few days of fruitless job-hunting, Riis hired on as a carpenter for an ironworks in Brady's Bend on the Allegheny River in upstate New York. Soon homesickness and the monotony of building huts for the miners overtook him. He tried his hand as a miner. He made more money, but the long back-breaking hours in the black pit proved too strenuous and he went back to carpentry. Unexpected news stirred him out of his melancholy: France had declared war on Germany. He thought that surely Denmark would join France to punish Prussia for stealing the Danish province of Schleswig in the War of 1864. "All the hot blood of youth was surging through me, I remembered the defeat, the humiliation of the flag I loved. . . ." He may also have seen the war as a way of getting home to see Elizabeth. He quickly sold some tools and clothes to buy a train ticket as far as Buffalo, where he pawned his trunk and watch to get to New York — with one cent in his pocket. In New York he walked straight to the French consulate to join the ranks, only to learn there were no plans to outfit a volunteer army in America nor funds for his transportation to France. At the Danish consulate the clerks could do no more than register him for military service in the event Denmark entered the war.

Dispirited and broke, Riis was again out on the streets. In order to square a previous account with a New York land-lady, he pawned his revolver and a pair of top boots. All he had now was a linen duster, an extra pair of socks and the prospect of sleeping on the street. At daybreak he set out for open country where a farmer might welcome a strong and willing hand. He walked all day and, exhausted and hungry, collapsed into an empty wagon to sleep. Before dawn the milkman who ran the wagon jerked him out of his slumber. He took a bath in a river and walked on, reaching Fordham College, where he wandered through the gates in a daze. A teacher, an old cleric in a cowl, invited him to breakfast — his first solid meal in days and the first time he had ever sat at ease with a Catholic priest.

Soon Riis was back in the city. For a while he had hoed cucumbers in exchange for meals and a haystack bed, but could find no job at decent pay. At least he wasn't broke; he had a silver quarter, the goodwill token of a young man who had come upon him sleeping in a wagon shed by the roadside. Now, glancing at the headlines in the New York *Sun,* Riis saw that the paper was helping recruit a regiment of volunteers to fight for France. He rushed to the *Sun* office, where he sought out the editor. The man shrugged his shoulders and said, "Editors sometimes do not know everything that is in their papers." Then, realizing that Riis looked hungry, he pulled out a dollar. "Go and get your breakfast; and better give up the war." Riis spurned the offer. "I came here to enlist, not to beg money for breakfast." He strode out of the office, proud and still hungry. The editor was the famous Charles Dana, and years later Riis would return as one of Dana's star reporters. After three unsuccessful attempts to fight for the French, Riis gave up the idea. Years later he rejoiced that fate had prevented him from joining the army that used a scapegoat for its own troubles when they charged a Jewish army captain named Dreyfus with spying for Germany. Dreyfus was subsequently exonerated and made a member of the Legion of Honor.

Riis carried with him letters of introduction to the Danish consul and to a businessman who was indebted to the

Riis family for saving his life in a shipwreck near Ribe. Earlier, Riis had called on both men but they were in Europe at the time. Now, when he needed help the most, he was too proud to try using the letters again and he destroyed them. He was also too proud to correspond with his family. He didn't want them — or Elizabeth — to know he was having such a hard time in America. "The city was full of idle men," he wrote later. "My last hope, a promise of employment in a human-hair factory failed, and homeless and pennyless I joined the great army of tramps, wandering about the streets in the daytime with one aim of somehow stilling the hunger that gnawed at my vitals, and fighting at night with vagrant curs or outcasts as miserable as myself for the protection of some sheltering ash-bin or doorway. I remember well a basement window at the downtown Delmonico's, the silent appearance of my ravenous face at which, at a certain hour of the evening, always evoked a generous supply of meat-bones and rolls from a white-capped cook who spoke French."

One morning, after a few excursions out of New York had convinced him he could do better elsewhere, Riis left the city vowing never to return. He followed the railroad tracks into western New York, where he found a more congenial atmosphere among the Scandinavians clustered in small towns there. He held jobs longer and his pay got better, enabling him to buy his first suit in America. On one job he contracted to plane and finish doors at 15 cents a door. In the first week Riis earned $15. When his employer realized that this was $5 more than Riis's predecessor had earned, he cut the price to 12 cents a door. The next week Riis worked extra hard and made $16. "The boss examined my work very carefully, said it was good, paid my wages, and cut the price to 10 cents. He did not want his men to earn more than $10 a week, saying it was not good for them." (Such exploitation was still prevalent fifty years later when I came to America. In 1923 I found a job in a large pencil factory. The company hired mostly immigrants — they would work for less pay and the fact that few spoke English made it difficult for them to organize into unions. One of the engineers, a countryman of mine, helped me become an overseer in the lead-cutting department. I showed the workers how to increase their production and earn higher wages under the piecework system. By the next week they had almost doubled their pay. Management then lowered the rate of pay — like Riis's employer — and thus became the sole beneficiary of my good intentions.)

Over the next two years Riis tried his hand at numerous occupations. He was carpenter, farm hand, common laborer, lumberjack, hunter and trapper, cabinetmaker, railroad hand, salesman. To break the boredom he felt in the small rural communities, he made his first tentative attempts as a lecturer and writer. In Jamestown, New York, he lectured to the local Scandinavians about astronomy and geology but got so bogged down in longitude and latitude that an old sea captain stood up to object and the entire audience walked out. "Other ambitions than to milk cows . . . were stirring in me," Riis wrote. "I had begun to write essays for the magazines, choosing for my topic the maltreatment of Denmark by Prussia, which ranked fresh in my memory, and the duty of all Scandinavians to rise up and avenge. The Scandinavians would not listen when I wrote in Danish, and my English outpourings never reached the publishers. I discovered that I lacked words — they didn't pour."

Nowhere in his diaries or books does Riis mention amorous encounters in the new land. Though he was a remarkable raconteur, there isn't a single tale about girls he might have liked. Perhaps his love for Elizabeth had sealed his heart against other girls. But he also kept before him a constant vision of his mother, who was the last to see him off on his journey to America. He had bidden her goodbye at the door of the wife of the miller, who comforted his mother by saying, "Jacob will come back President of the United States." Riis enjoyed the comradeship of men, but he worshiped women, whom he put on a higher plane than men. Many years later, when his oldest daughter became engaged to be married, Riis was overcome by hopelessness at the prospect of losing her.

Of his many jobs during this period, Riis was most successful as a salesman. After several good months of peddling flat and fluting irons, he was made factory representative for the State of Illinois. He hired subagents to help him cover the huge territory. The enterprise looked good — orders were mounting — but in Chicago Riis ran afoul of local sharpies. Among them were some of his childhood chums, who had immigrated from Denmark. "In six weeks they had cleaned me out bodily, had run away with my irons and with money they borrowed of me to start them in business. I returned to Pittsburgh as poor as ever, to find that the agents I had left behind in my Pennsylvania territory had dealt with me after the same fashion. The firm for which I worked had contrived at the frauds. My friends had left me."

Down and out once more, Riis wandered up the Allegheny River where he fell ill with fever. Bedridden in a riverside tavern, he received the worst blow of all. A letter from home that had been forwarded to him announced that Elizabeth was engaged to be married to a cavalry officer. "In all my misadventures that was the one thing I had never dreamed of," he wrote. "That she should be another's bride seemed so utterly impossible. . . . At the thought I turned my face to the wall and hoped that I might die."

In this lonely tavern, toward the end of his third year in America, Riis nursed himself back in health and heart. Then, on foot, he started his slow trek back East, peddling flatirons to pay his way. Later he would remark that at twenty-four one does not die of a broken heart.

Chapter 3

"Noblest of All the Callings"

When he reached New York after spending the entire summer on the trip East, Riis's wanderlust was ebbing. He decided to seek a permanent job and invested all his money in a training course for telegraphers. Before completing the course, however, he turned again to an ambition he apparently had harbored for some time — perhaps since his boyhood days when he helped his father with newspaper work. "It seemed to me that a reporter was the highest and noblest of all the callings," he wrote later, "no one could sift wrong from right as he, and punish the wrong. . . ." Once before, while knocking around the state, he had dropped into a newspaper office in Buffalo to apply for a job. "What are you?" asked the editor. "A carpenter," replied Riis. The editor laughed in his face and pushed him out of the office. "You laugh," shouted Riis, shaking his fist, "but wait . . ." Riis wrote, "In that hour it was settled that I was to be a reporter."

Now, seeing a classified ad placed by a small Long Island weekly, Riis skipped telegraphy class and rushed to the newspaper. He got the job, city editor. Afterward he learned that the job was usually open because the editor in chief was dishonest, a scandalmonger and heavily in debt. After two weeks Riis quit, forfeiting his pay. Broke, but having endured a brief baptism in journalism, he returned to his old haunts in the Five Points section of downtown New York. The area had long been notorious at home and abroad as a place of misery, degradation and lawlessness. Thirty years earlier, Charles Dickens had vividly described Five Points:

This is the place; these narrow ways, diverging to the right and to the left, and reeking everywhere with dirt and filth. . . . The coarse and bloated faces at the doors have counterparts at home. . . . Debauchery has made the very houses prematurely old. See how the rotten beams are tumbling down and how the patched and broken windows seem to scowl dimly, like eyes that have been hurt in drunken frays. Many of the pigs live here. Do they ever wonder why their masters walk upright in lieu of going on all-fours? Where dogs would howl to lie, women and men and boys slink off to sleep, forcing the dislodged rats to move away in quest of better lodgings. Here too . . . are . . . hideous tenements which take their name from robbery and murder; all that is loathsome, drooping and decayed is here.

By Riis's time little had changed. A contemporary author noted the appalling statistics: "Forty thousand vagrant and destitute children . . . too dirty, too ragged . . . to be admitted to the public schools. Over a thousand young girls, between the ages of twelve and eighteen, can be found in the Water Street drinking saloons . . . children can be seen who come up daily from the brothels and dens of infamy which they call their homes." Many of the lodging houses were underground, without ventilation; lodgers slept on canvas bags filled with rotten straw, which they rented for five or ten cents a night. Riis himself spent many nights in the police lodging cellars, which were free. The misery of his existence in Five Points cannot be discounted, and yet he was drawn to it again and again. For him Five Points proved to be a kind of hard-knocks school of journalism.

One day he was sitting disconsolately on the steps of the Cooper Institute. He was back where he had begun three years before, broke, hungry and now, "bankrupt in hope and purpose." In his hand was a copy of the new Dickens book *Hard Times*, which he had been futilely attempting to peddle door to door. The principal of his telegraphy school happened by and saw him. He glanced at the title of the book and snorted: "Books . . . I guess they won't make you rich. Now how would you like to be a reporter if you have nothing better to do? News Agency's manager asked me today to find him a bright young fellow whom he could break in. It isn't much — $10 a week to start with. But it is better than peddling books, I know."

Riis spent another night on the streets, rose early, washed up at a horse-watering trough and rushed to the New York News Association where the editor looked up incredulously at the rumpled young man. But he was impressed by Riis's willingness to begin work so early and told him to wait. At 10 A.M. he was sent on the first assignment of the day, covering a luncheon at the Astor House. Three days without food must have sharpened his perception: despite the distraction of the savory meal being served, he submitted a good report and got the job. "That night, when I was dismissed from the office, I went up the Bowery . . . where a Danish family kept a boardinghouse up under the roof. I had work and wages now, and could pay. On the stairs I fell in a swoon and lay there till someone stumbled over me in the dark and carried me in. My strength had at last given out. So began my life as a newspaper man."

This first job of collecting general news wherever it happened gave Riis the chance to get acquainted with parts of the city beyond his familiar tenement district. New York, already America's chief financial and cultural center, had 11,000 factories devoted to clothing, cigars, furniture and printing. Millionaires from all over the country came there to live in the magnificent edifices along Fifth and Madison avenues. Its seaport drew 30,000 ships annually and was the gateway for the immigrants — German, Swedish, Norwegian and Danish, Irish, Italian, Jewish, French — with whom Riis felt at home. The immigrants tended to settle among their own kind where they could find cheap lodgings and home-operated sweatshops. They struggled to make a better life for their children, many of whom grew up to become, like Riis, celebrated citizens of the new land.

Riis wrote about pushcart vendors who lost their profits to police graft, about sweatshop slaves, about homeless boys. Writing came easy to him, even though English was not his native tongue. No literary stylist, he had the storytelling gift of a homespun narrator. He worked sixteen hours a day. Any time now, he expected to hear from home that Elizabeth was married and a "furious kind of energy took possession of me at the mere idea."

He earned a reputation as a good reporter and soon accepted the title of editor and a higher salary on a small local weekly. It turned out that the *News* was a front for a group of politicians and heavily in debt. Just as the debt-ridden paper was going out of business — it was Christmas Eve — a letter arrived from Riis's father. Never since Riis had left home had a letter from his family reached him in time for Christmas, his favorite holiday. This one bore extraordinary news. His two older brothers and a favorite aunt had died. Riis wept. But the most important tidings were saved for the postscript: Elizabeth's fiancé, too, had died. In the next few days new hope of having Elizabeth surged unashamedly through him. He wrote her a long letter pouring out his feelings. Then, with his savings, $75, and some promissory notes, he purchased the assets of the *News*.

"The *News* was a big four-page sheet," he recalled. "Literally every word in it I wrote myself. I was my own editor, reporter, publisher and advertising agent. In the early morning hours I shouldered the edition and carried it down to the ferry. . . . When I got home, I slept on the counter with the edition for my pillow, in order to be up with the first gleam of daylight to skirmish for newsboys."

In five months he saved enough to pay off his debts on the paper. No longer financially obligated to the politicians, he became their scourge. Finally, the politicians bought him off with a sinecure as a court interpreter. He continued to publish his paper but toned down his attacks. He had Elizabeth on his mind and didn't want to jeopardize their future together. For the rest of his life, Riis regretted his weakness in giving in to the political bosses. Though he was asked many times to be a public official, he never again accepted.

It was agonizing months before he received Elizabeth's reply: she was willing to go with him to America if he would come for her. He answered immediately that he would be back in Denmark within a year. Then came another stroke of luck. The politicians wanted to buy back the *News*. They gave him five times the price he had paid for it, and Riis took the next steamer for home. He had left Denmark with $40; he was coming back a hundred times richer. When he arrived in Ribe, Elizabeth's palatial home at last opened its doors to the one-time carpenter boy. Three months later Elizabeth and Jacob were married. "I hear people saying . . . there is no such thing as luck," Riis often said. "They are wrong. There is; I know it. It runs in streaks, like accidents and fires. The thing is to get in the way of it and keep there till it comes along, then hitch on, and away you go."

When Riis arrived in New York with his bride, America was in the grip of another depression. With his savings to fall back on, he and Elizabeth busied themselves with the pleasant task of setting up housekeeping in a small Danish neighborhood in Brooklyn. At length, he hired himself out to edit the newspaper of a south Brooklyn political machine but couldn't stomach it for long. Then, looking around for another means of livelihood, he hit upon an idea that was to impress upon him, perhaps for the first time, the immense power of the visual image. Some time before, he had bought at a rummage sale a magic lantern, an early version of today's slide projector. The device could project enlarged images of slides—either photographic transparencies or pictures painted on glass in transparent watercolors—and Riis thought it might provide entertainment for his future chil-

dren. It first came into use at the end of the seventeenth century — for amusement, anatomical lectures and even to dupe the superstitious.

Riis brought out his magic lantern from basement storage and launched a highly innovative advertising scheme. He started modestly, projecting ads for neighborhood merchants on a sheet stretched between two trees. When cold weather came, he moved into an empty store and flashed his pictures onto a screen in the window. His shows attracted large crowds of fascinated viewers. He shrewdly interspersed the ads with beautiful scenic views. "I advertised nothing I would not have sold the people myself, and I gave it to them in the way that was distinctly pleasing and good for them; for my pictures were real works of art, not the cheap trash you see nowadays on street screens."

Successful in Brooklyn, Riis and a friend decided to take their advertising business to small towns. In upstate New York and western Pennsylvania they moved from town to town with nightly displays. After several months of thriving, the operation ended when Riis and his partner got caught unwittingly in the violence between the law and a group of striking railroad workers. "I heard a word of brief command, the rattle of a score of guns . . . and a volley was fired into the crowd point blank. A man beside me weltered in his blood. There was an instant's dead silence, then the rushing of a thousand feet and the cries of terror as the mob broke and fled. We ran with it. In all my life I never ran so fast."

Jobless again, and now with a baby to support, Riis ran into one of those happy coincidences he liked to remark upon. One of his neighbors happened to be the city editor of the New York *Tribune*. Through his recommendation Riis got a job as a probationary reporter. All that winter he covered news, mostly on foot, for long hours at little pay. Just as he was about to look for a better job, his boss offered him an assignment as a police reporter. The editor told him: "It is a place that needs a man who will run to get his copy in, tell the truth and stick to it. You will find plenty of fighting there. But don't go knocking people down, unless you have to." Riis ran to the telegraph office to send Elizabeth the news: GOT STAFF APPOINTMENT. POLICE HEADQUARTERS. TWENTY-FIVE DOLLARS A WEEK. HURRAH!

At first the press office, across the street from police headquarters on Mulberry Street, gave Riis a cold reception. The other reporters thought him overly ambitious; they went at their work leisurely, taking turns gathering the news and then sharing it with all. After Riis achieved several scoops, they accepted him and soon nicknamed him "the boss reporter." Riis wrote: "Of the advantages that smoothed the way to newsgetting, I had none. I was a stranger, and I was never distinguished for detective ability. But good hard work goes a long way toward making up for lack of genius."

Mulberry Street, around which Riis was to spend a quarter of a century, was nicknamed "Death's Thoroughfare." It was here, where the street crooks its elbow at the Five Points, that the streets and numerous alleys radiated in all directions, forming the foul core of the New York slums. Until about 1767 Mulberry Street was a path lined with mulberry trees over which cows with tinkling bells came home from pasture. The old people still remembered scavenger pigs roaming the neighborhood; now the tinkling bells proclaimed the homecoming of ragpickers. There is a negative in the Riis Collection of a yard behind an ancient homestead. It is inscribed: "The Last Mulberry. It isn't. It is probably an old Ailanthus."

Riis doubted his ability to last on the police beat. The hours were late, and Elizabeth waited up for him, homesick for Denmark and singing to keep up her courage. After a year he asked for a transfer. The editor refused, saying that Riis was irreplaceable. "Go back and stay," he said. "Unless I'm much mistaken you are finding something there that needs you."

For the next ten years Riis kept at it, investigating, absorbing, writing, hammering away at indifference and graft. Walter Lippmann once remarked: "The rewards in journalism go to specialty work . . . to men with a knack and flavor of their own. If he sees a building with a dangerous list, he

does not have to wait until it falls into the street." Riis was just that kind of journalist: he didn't wait for the building to fall before he probed its rotting foundation. The range of his reportorial interests is revealed in this sampling of headlines from his scrapbook for the years 1883–87: VIRUS FARM, REMOVING THE DEAD, EPIDEMIC DANGERS, CUTE TRICKS OF THIEVES, MEN WITH PISTOLS, RED TAPE EXTRAVAGANCE, WHAT IT COSTS TO KEEP RATS, A CHURCH WITH A NEW IDEA.

He was accused of being one-sided, of prejudice, of overemphasizing certain facts. In the end he was virtually always vindicated. He didn't despise the rich, nor even criticize them. He only criticized poverty. Years later, when a Russian theoretical anarchist, Prince Peter Kropotkin, complimented him for his relentless exposure of social conditions in America and called him a revolutionary, Riis retorted: "I don't like the Reds." At every opportunity he stepped out of the slum to solicit support from people of influence and financial standing. John Haynes Holmes observed: "What moved Riis most was the spectacle of helpless human beings robbed of their sheer joy of living which was his own richest treasure."

Others were exposing the seamy side of New York life, but their writings exploited the slums for profit. Books filled with advice to visitors on where to go for slumming and adventure bore such titles as *Sunshine and Shadow*, *Darkness and Daylight* and *Light and Darkness*. The text in such books was enhanced with artists' drawings that made the narration more vivid. Riis also felt the need for pictorial documentation of his stories. He tried his own hand at drawing the scenes he reported, but had to admit he was a poor artist. Besides, he knew that the line drawings of even the most skilled artist could not convey the impact of what he saw and wished to document. Aware that words were not enough, he was "frustrated, dissatisfied and anxious. . . . In anger I looked around for something to strike off . . . fetters with. But there was nothing." Then, when he least expected it, the tool he desperately needed presented itself.

Chapter 4

Light for the Darkest Corner

Jacob Riis had never even thought of buying a camera, much less using one to record the misery his own eyes saw with such righteous anger. It was a slow, cumbersome instrument, built for the brightness of day; what Riis wanted to expose cowered in dark tenements. Then, early in the spring of 1887, four lines of newspaper type brought Riis his flash of light. "One morning scanning my newspaper at the breakfast table, I put it down with an outcry that startled my wife sitting opposite. There it was, the thing I had been looking for all these years. A four-line dispatch from somewhere in Germany, if I remember right, had it all. A way had been discovered, it ran, to take pictures by flashlight. The darkest corner might be photographed that way."

The new method was a forerunner of the modern flash gun, a pistol lamp that fired magnesium cartridges to provide light for instantaneous unposed photographs. Riis immediately saw its potential for his own crusades and told his friend Dr. John Nagle, an enthusiastic amateur photographer who was chief of the Bureau of Vital Statistics in the City Health Department. Nagle enlisted a couple of other amateur photographers. With Riis in the lead, they began a series of nighttime forays into the slums — armed with cameras and the new pistol lamp. The drama of these bizarre expeditions was vividly described by Riis some months later in an unsigned article that appeared in the New York *Sun* on February 12, 1888. It was the first published account of the use of the new technique in America.

Flashes from the Slums
Pictures taken in dark places by the

Lighting Process
Some of the Results of a Journey Through the City
with an Instantaneous Camera—
The Poor, the Idle and the Vicious.

With their way illuminated by spasmodic flashes, as bright and sharp and brief as those of the lightning itself, a mysterious party has lately been startling the town o'nights. Somnolent policemen on the street, denizens of the dives in their dens, tramps and bummers in their so-called lodgings, and all the people of the wild and wonderful variety of New York night life have in their turn marvelled at and been frightened by the phenomenon. What they saw was three or four figures in the gloom, a ghostly tripod, some weird and uncanny movements, the blinding flash, and then they heard the patter of retreating footsteps, and the mysterious visitors were gone before they could collect their scattered thoughts and try to find out what it was all about. Of course, all this fuss speedily became known to the Sun reporters, and equally as a matter of course they speedily found out the meaning of the seeming mystery. But at the request of the parties interested the publication of the facts was delayed until the purpose of the expedition was accomplished. That has now been done, and its history may now be written.

The party consisted of members of the Society of Amateur Photographers of New York experimenting with the process of taking instantaneous pictures by an artificial flashlight and their guide and conductor, an energetic gentleman, who combines in his person, though not in practise, the two dignities of deacon in a Long Island church and a police reporter in New York. His object in the matter, besides the interest in the taking of the pictures, was the collection of a series of views for magic lantern slides, showing, as no mere de-

scription could, the misery and vice that he had noticed in his ten years of experience. Aside from its strong human interest, he thought that this treatment of the topic would call attention to the needs of the situation, and suggest the direction in which much good might be done. The nature of this feature of the deacon-reporter's idea is indicated by the way he has succeeded on Long Island in the work of helping the destitute children of the metropolis. The ground about the little church edifice is turned into a garden, in which the Sunday school children work at spading, hoeing, planting, and weeding, and the potatoes and other vegetables thus raised are contributed to a children's home in the city. In furtherance of such aims the deacon-reporter threw himself with tireless energy into the pursuit of pictures of Gotham's crime and misery by night and day to make a foundation for a lecture called "The Other Half: How it Lives and Dies in New York," to give at church and Sunday school exhibitions, and the like.

The entire composition of the night rousing party was: Dr. Henry G. Piffard and Richard Hoe Lawrence, two accomplished and progressive Amateur Photographers; Dr. John T. Nagle of the Health Board, who is strongly interested in the same direction, and Jacob A. Riis, the deacon-reporter. . . . Mr. Riis kindly furnished a number of his photographs to the Sun artist and they are given here.

The article was accompanied by twelve line drawings based on photographs taken by Riis's companions — then the newspaper's accepted way of reproducing pictures. His amateur photographers were fascinated by the flashlight process but soon tired of the late-night hours. Riis next tried hiring professionals. One, an *Evening Sun* employee named Collins, was too slow to suit Riis. The other photographer was in all probability A. D. Fisk, who had a studio at 18 Ann Street. Riis wrote of the second photographer: "He was even less willing to get up at 2 a.m. than my friends, who had a good excuse. He had none, for I paid him well. He repaid me by trying to sell my photographs behind my back." Riis went to court and established that he owned the negatives — probably a precedent in winning for an employer the rights to pictures taken for him. It cost Riis a lawyer's fee of $15, no

small amount then. Riis later wrote this footnote to his exasperating experiences with the photographer: "He was a pious man, I take it, for when I tried to have him photograph the waifs in the baby nursery at the Five Points House of Industry, as they were saying their 'Now I lay me down to sleep,' and the plate came out blank the second time, he owned up that it was his doing: it went against his principles to take a picture of anyone at prayers. The spectacle of a man prevented by religious scruples from photographing children at prayers, while plotting at the same time to rob his employer, has been a kind of chart to me that has piloted me through more than one quagmire of queer human nature. Nothing could stump me after that."

Riis again sought help from his friend Dr. Nagle, who suggested the obvious. So, in January 1888, Riis bought a camera, loaded the plateholders and went to Potter's Field on Hart Island to experiment. On that cold morning there were no burials and no one in sight to distract him. He trained his camera on an open trench and made two exposures. Then he made his first error as a photographer: he put the two exposed plates back among the other ten plates he had brought and thus had to develop all twelve to get one picture. His photograph of the snow-covered common grave was much overexposed, but dramatically right to accentuate the feeling of desolation in a paupers' cemetery.

The entire photographic outfit cost him $25. It consisted of a 4 × 5 wooden box camera, the plateholders, a tripod, a safety lantern, developing trays and a printing frame. By this time a safer and less startling flashlight technique had replaced the pistol lamps brandished by Riis's earlier raiding parties. ("Our party carried terror wherever it went," Riis observed. "The spectacle of strange men invading a house in the mid-night hours armed with pistols which they shot off recklessly was hardly reassuring . . . and it was not to be wondered at if the tenants bolted through the windows and down fire-escapes.") The pistol lamp cartridges contained highly explosive chemicals, which had seriously burned several photographers. The newer method, developed by Armstrong of London late in 1887, used magnesium powder blown through an alcohol flame. Riis ignited the powder on a frying pan. "It seemed more homelike," he explained. Even so, Riis once blew the light into his own eyes and only his glasses saved him from being blinded for life.

The circumstances of Riis's photography make the resulting pictures all the more remarkable. Unlike modern flash systems, his home-rigged frying pan device was not synchronized with the camera. He had to remove the cap from his lens, quickly ignite the flash powder, then replace the cap. Some of his pictures show a slight blur — movement of his subjects just before the firing of the powder. Once, Riis set fire to a tenement room and, because the tenants were blind, had to smother the blaze by himself. He also faced obstacles more familiar to documentary photographers today. He and his camera were driven off by a band of angry women who pelted him with stones. A tramp accepted 10 cents to pose for a picture, then demanded a quarter when Riis asked him to put his clay pipe back in his mouth. Other subjects insisted on posing when Riis wanted a candid picture. A group of young ruffians who called themselves "the Montgomery Guards" set up an elaborate tableau to show how they picked pockets: one of them slouched against a shed to simulate the sleeping victim while two others ransacked his pockets. Riis's lament about subject-staged pictures would be echoed by future legions of documentary photographers: "Their determination to be 'took' the moment the camera hove into sight, in the most striking pose that they could hastily devise, was always the most formidable bar to success I met."

Riis time and again expressed wonderment at the process by which an image emerged from apparent nothing. "To watch the picture come out upon the plate that was blank before, and that saw with me for perhaps the merest fraction of a second, maybe a month before, the thing it has never forgotten, is a new miracle every time. If I were a clergyman . . . I would preach about it." Most of all, Riis marveled at the practical impact of his pictures. Truth had previously boiled down to the reporter's word against someone else's; in the courts the only pictorial evidence was in the form of artists' sketches, which often were ruled out because such drawings relied on faulty memory and the bias of the human imagination. Now Riis had the most tangible proof to back his allegations. Few listened when he reported that tenement lodgers slept fifteen to a room; his pictures proved it. When typhus broke out in the city, he warned that the police lodging rooms were ripe for it; he photographed the effects of typhus in these crowded dens and took his pictures directly to the Academy of Medicine to alert the doctors. From his pictures, "there was no appeal."

When Riis had enough pictures to illustrate several articles, he began making the rounds of magazine publishers. At Harper's he ran into one of those unhappy ironies of the trade: the editor liked the pictures and offered to buy them, but he wanted someone else "who could write" to do the article.

Riis was so disheartened that he stopped his extracurricular writing attempts and sought another forum — speaking at church meetings. As soon as the churches learned he was a Mulberry Street police reporter, they turned him down. Some churches thought his tales of slum life would be offensive to parishioners; others derived considerable income from their ownership of tumble-down tenements. It was true even of the most fashionable Trinity Corporation, which managed the endowment properties. "[They] held delapidated rookeries, so they were called, vile tenement blocks, for rental to the poor. These were dark close-built 'old law' cold-water housings, in the 'long blocks'. . . . Many children went heavenward from the dark damp hovels." Riis's own church on Long Island prevented him from delivering an address there and he angrily resigned from the diaconate. Then he met two prominent churchmen, Dr. Adolph Schauffler, superintendent of the City Mission Society, and

Dr. Josiah Strong, whose book *Our Country* was a pioneer work in sociology. The two men were impressed by his photographs and plans and agreed to sponsor his lecture at the Broadway Tabernacle, a progressive church long famous for its antislavery meetings.

Riis had only a few weeks to have lantern slides prepared from his negatives for the lecture, and he had practically no money. The upkeep on his family was growing — he and Elizabeth now had four children — and he had recently gone in debt to build their new house in Richmond Hill on Long Island. To purchase the land alone, he had been forced to take part-time work revising Danish insurance policies. The manager of the Press Bureau for which Riis worked put up the money for the construction of the house and took a mortgage on the entire cost. Behind the house Riis built a charming writer's study that looked like a dollhouse. Though the children were instructed that "Papa is not to be disturbed," the children found reasons to invade his privacy. Without admitting it, he delighted in their visits. Riis wanted a house and lawn for every child in New York. He wrote that his secret wish was "to go around and pay off mortgages on the little homes, so that the owners when they had got the interest together by pinching and scraping should find it all gone and paid up without knowing how." To help finance his new lecture enterprise, he took a partner. He was Riis's friend W. L. Craig, a Health Department clerk who paid all the bills for several months.

The lecture at the Broadway Tabernacle was a huge success — except in the pocketbook of the new partnership. Riis and Craig received nothing. The Mission Society netted $143.50. "I had my say and felt better," Riis wrote. But the $143.50 in proceeds provoked a flash of grim humor — "The fifty cents would have come in handy for lunch that day." The expense accounts kept by Riis and his partner indicate how little they profited from the early lectures: "Jamaica Town Hall, March 7 — 32.50; Plymouth Church, April 12 — 46; Lexington Avenue Baptist Church, April 26 — 25." On June 28, 1888, Riis summed up the accounts: "Expenses of entire business 219.69, deduct amount paid 116.50. Leaves to pay Craig 103.19. Understanding fixed that ½ of all net income goes to Craig until full outlay is paid. Thenceforth he receives a one fourth and owns a one fourth interest in the concern and all that comes from it in any way."

The lectures proved immensely profitable in other ways. They gave him large new audiences for his message and the occasion to meet and form lasting friendships with such celebrated reformers as Dr. Charles Parkhurst, the crusading clergyman who later helped beat Tammany Hall. Riis's lantern slides electrified his audiences. He already knew the selling power of visual images — from his magic lantern advertising venture and from his early days as a traveling salesman when he took along an album of pictures to clinch his sales of furniture. Now pictures and the spoken word were selling his deepest convictions about human misery. "Almost before I knew it, my tongue was enlisted in the fight as well as my pen and the pictures. . . . I lay no claims to eloquence. So it must have been the facts."

Among the listeners and viewers at a Riis illustrated lecture was an editor of the influential *Scribner's* magazine. He was so moved by the story of "bitter poverty, of landlord's greed, of sweatshop slavery, of darkness and squalor and misery" that he asked Riis to submit an article with pictures. The story, titled "How the Other Half Lives," appeared in *Scribner's* at Christmas 1889. The layout covered eighteen pages and carried no less than nineteen of Riis's photographs converted into line drawings. It was the first time his photographs appeared in a national publication. The extraordinary number of pictures used by the magazine — high engraving costs ordinarily limited illustrations to a handful — was a tribute to their unique power.

The article was a breakthrough. A few days later Riis came home to find a letter from a magazine writer suggesting he expand the article into a book — she knew a publisher who might be interested. Riis was jubilant, but his wife looked troubled. Riis wrote: "I saw a tear in her eye as she bent over the baby's cradle. 'Shall we lose you now?' she whispered and hid her head on my shoulder. I don't know what jealous thoughts of authors being wedded to their work had come into her mind. . . . I registered a vow which I have kept. It was the last tear she shed for me."

Actually the idea for the book came to Riis at a meeting of ministers of every sect who were concerned about the losing fight the church was waging among the masses when a man cried out, "How are these men and women to understand the love of God you speak of when they see only the greed of men?" Riis wrote, "I wanted to jump up in my seat at that time and shout Amen! But I remembered that I was a reporter and kept still. It was that same winter, however, that I wrote the title of my book . . . and copyrighted it. The book itself did not come out until two years after, but it was as good as written then. I had my text."

Riis began his first book within weeks after the *Scribner's* article. Sensing that the popularity of the article might be partly attributable to its catchy title, he chose the same title for the book. It was an abbreviation of the one he copyrighted as: "The Other Half, how it lives and dies in New York, with 100 illustrations, photographs from real life, of the haunts of poverty and vice in a great city." The writing put a tremendous strain on him. His duties as a reporter — he had switched from the *Tribune* to the *Sun* in November 1890 — took up the days; his lectures took up many of the evenings. He wrote late at night, a regimen that left him so exhausted that one evening at a friend's house, when the maid asked him who he was, he could not remember his own name. Thereafter he never left home without a calling card in his pocket.

The book was published in late 1890, ten months after he began writing. The text was tough, biting, aimed at the conscience of America. Photographically, *How the Other Half Lives* was a landmark — the first account of social conditions to be documented with action pictures. It was also apparently the first book to use a large number of pictures reproduced by the new halftone process. The book used seventeen halftones, in addition to the eighteen line drawings reproduced earlier in the *Scribner's* article. (Strangely, this fact went unnoticed in Robert Taft's account of the first use of halftones in *Photography and the American Scene*, which mentions books published in 1890 and 1891 that carried only a few halftones. In fact, the first large-scale use of halftones occurred in a picture magazine, *Sun and Shade*, which began publication in July 1888 and had to abandon the practice a year later because of the high costs.)

Riis's first book went into several editions and was widely quoted from the pulpit. Magazine critics praised it, some with reservations. "His aim is to let us know the worst," said the liberal weekly *The Nation*, "and it is not surprising that special emphasis should be laid upon whatever intensifies the darkness, but he allows us at least to see that there is another side." *The Critic*, whose staff member had originally suggested the book to Riis, was less enthusiastic: "His book is literally a photograph and as such has its value and a lesson, but also serious limitations. There is a lack of broad and penetrating vision, a singularly warped sense of justice at times, and a roughness amounting almost to brutality." Some reformers, such as Ellen Collins, a prominent worker in the better housing movement, objected that Riis had painted an overly dark portrait. Riis agreed, but like another great muckraker, Lincoln Steffens, he believed that readers would often accept an ironical statement of facts they might otherwise reject. Wrote Riis: "There is a standing quarrel between the official sanitarian and the unsalaried agitator for sanitary reform over the question of overcrowded tenements. The one puts the number a little vaguely at four or five hundred, while the other asserts that there are thirty-two thousand. . . . It depends on the angle from which one sees it. . . ."

Riis believed that the popular success of his book was due in part to interest in reform aroused by a recent exposé of London's slums, *In Darkest England and the Way Out* by

Charles Booth. He also felt that another, quite different book helped draw attention to his own work: Samuel Ward McAllister's *Society As I Have Found It,* a flippant saga of the other "other half"—New York's very wealthy.

Other publishers attempted to capitalize on the popularity of the new documentary approach. One such book published in 1892, *Darkness and Daylight; or Lights and Shadows of New York Life,* carried at least eleven photographs from the present Riis Collection. These included Murderers' Row in the Tombs Prison, opium dens in Chinatown and other scenes that were out of bounds to those who, unlike Riis, did not have the privileged access of a police reporter. Though the book's preface hailed the new technique of flashlight photography — paraphrasing Riis's old *Sun* article — it failed even to mention Riis's role in establishing the method in America. Most of the pictures in the book were obviously taken in daylight; the preface asserted many were taken by flashlight. A further irony was the sermon-like introduction written by Rev. Lymen Abbott, who was both pastor of the Plymouth Church, where Riis had given one of his first illustrated lectures, and editor of the magazine *Outlook,* which later published some thirty-five articles by Riis. The book's text turned out to be just another attempt to titillate a thrill-seeking audience. One of its authors was the superintendent of the New York police detective bureau, a Mulberry Street colleague about whom Riis had decidedly mixed feelings. "Byrnes stood for the old days that were bad," Riis wrote. "He was unscrupulous, he was for Byrnes — he was a policeman, in short, with all the failings of the trade."

Riis's first book proved there was an audience that was genuinely concerned about social conditions. Publishers clamored for more and Riis responded with a sequel. *The Children of the Poor* was published in 1892 and dedicated to his own children: "May the love that shines in their eager eyes never grow cold within them; then they shall yet grow up to give a helping hand in working out this problem which so plagues the world today." The book related individual case histories from Riis's firsthand knowledge and contained a comprehensive list of charitable institutions helping to care for children. Thanks in part to photography, Riis now had a promising new career as an author. He also had a new alliance with a fast-rising young political star, one that would help thrust Riis into the forefront of reform across the nation.

Chapter 5

"The Most Useful Citizen"

Shortly after the publication of his first book, *How the Other Half Lives*, Riis found on his office desk a card bearing the name Theodore Roosevelt. On the back of the card, hastily scribbled, was a one-line message saying that Roosevelt had read the book and had come to help. Years later Riis wrote, "The message was short, but it told the whole story of a man. I loved him from the day I first saw him; not ever in all the years that have passed has he failed of the promise made then. No one ever helped as he did."

Roosevelt was then just coming into political prominence. He and Riis began a friendship that followed Roosevelt's rise: president of New York City's police board, governor of New York, vice-president, president of the United States. The two men shared many of the same characteristics: personal honesty, uncompromising stubbornness, a decisiveness in seeing things through. They also were both Republicans, though Riis seldom participated in partisan politics. Originally a Democrat, he switched parties because of the corruption of Tammany Hall.

In May 1895 Roosevelt was appointed president of the city police board and began making good on his promise to Riis. He immediately asked Riis to guide him on a midnight inspection tour of police posts. On their first round they found nine out of ten patrolmen missing from their posts. Riis whipped up a story about it for the next day's paper. As a result, the entire police force woke up and stayed awake for the next two years, the duration of Roosevelt's term. During one of their middle-of-the-night tours, Riis took Roosevelt to the lodging rooms at the Church Street police station. There he told his friend the story of the most traumatic experience

of his life, which had occurred at this station some twenty-five years before. The story he told already had been recounted several years before in a full-page article in the *Tribune*, "Vice Which Is Unchecked." Riis was both the author of the piece and the "poor boy" who is the victim in this story within a story. The article first describes a recent visit of two distinguished English women to the lodging rooms of the Church Street station. After painting the horrors of the lodging rooms in fulsome detail, Riis gets to the point of his story:

The ladies turned away with loathing, after a brief look. "Is it possible," said Lady Summerset to her conductor, "for a man to sleep there a night and come out a decent, self-respecting being?" "Once, yes!" said he drily, and as they went upstairs he told them this story: "One rainy October night in the year 1870, a poor boy sat on the bulwark down by the river, hungry, footsore and drenched to the skin. He sat thinking of friends and home thousands of miles away over the sea, whom he had left six months before to go alone among strangers. He had been alone ever since, but never more so than that night. His money gone, no work to be found, he had slept in the streets for nights, too proud to appeal in his wretchedness to those who could and would help him for the sake of those over there. That day he had eaten nothing; he would die rather than beg. And one of the two he must do soon. There was the dark river, rushing at his feet; the swirl of the unseen waters whispered to him of rest and peace – it was so cold – and who was there to care, he thought bitterly. No one who would ever know. He moved a little nearer the edge, and listened more intently. Just then a little whine fell on his ear, and a cold wet face was pressed against him; a little black and tan dog that had been crouching beside him, settled in his lap. It was his only friend. He had picked it up in the street, as forlorn as himself, and it had stuck to him. Its touch recalled him to himself. He got up hastily and taking the dog in his arms went to this same police station and asked for shelter. It was the first time he had accepted even such charity, and as he lay down on his hard plank in that room downstairs he hugged a little gold locket he wore around his neck, the last link with better days, and thought with a hard dry sob of home.

When he awoke the next morning, the locket was gone. One of the tramps who slept with him had stolen it. He went up and complained to the sergeant at the desk and the sergeant ordered him to be kicked out in the street as a liar, if not a thief. How should a tramp boy have come honestly by a gold locket? The doorman put him out as he was bidden, and when the little dog showed his teeth a policeman seized it and clubbed it to death there on the step.

"And the boy?" said one of the ladies when the story was told. "He went out to battle with the world and to conquer," was the reply. "He lived to become a useful man. That one night in the police station cured him of dreaming."

Now, as Riis related the long tale to Roosevelt, his friend turned red with anger. "Did they do that to you?" Roosevelt asked. Then he brought his clenched fists together. "I will smash them tomorrow." Roosevelt closed the police lodging rooms in February 1896, and in a single stroke ended Riis's years of battling these infamous holes. "Among all the things which I have been credited with," wrote Riis, "it is one of the few in which I really bore a strong hand. And yet it was not mine which finally wrought that great work, but a stronger and better than mine, Theodore Roosevelt's . . . we together drove in the last nail in the coffin of the bad old days."

The only time Riis may have had second thoughts about his relationship with Roosevelt came later, during the days preceding the outbreak of the Spanish-American War. When rumors began to fly that the United States planned to stop Spain's mistreatment of the Cubans, some liberal groups ap-

proached Riis to investigate the situation. They believed that the real instigators of the coming conflict were the U.S. Naval authorities looking for a pretext to seize a strategic island lying near the Caribbean ports on the path to the projected Panama Canal. Riis wrote to his sister: "I had a very good offer . . . and it would have brought me about $150 a week. . . . A large part of our population, especially in New England, do not think the war against Spain is just. The Universities, especially disapprove. It would have been my work to find out the truth and write about it." He declined to accept any position offered him, saying he did not wish to become involved in politics. He was glad when his two sons, for physical reasons, were prevented from entering the war. The Cuban campaign wrecked Riis's career as a foreign correspondent when the Danish papers took opposite views to the American attitude. Riis was accused of being overpatriotic in his youthful enthusiasm. He retorted, "The bottom fact was the distrust of the United States that was based upon a curiously stubborn ignorance, entirely without excuse in a people of high intelligence like Danes." At the start of the war Theodore Roosevelt began outfitting a company of volunteers, the "Rough Riders," and asked Riis to help him. Riis performed routine tasks, but declined to be an official.

Later, when Roosevelt succeeded to the presidency after the assassination of William McKinley in 1901, Riis became a frequent visitor to the White House. He was known as a personal friend of the president, a reputation that opened many doors otherwise barred to an investigative reporter. Roosevelt wrote a stirring tribute to his friend, saying in part:

Recently a man, well qualified to pass judgment, alluded to Mr. Jacob A. Riis as "the most useful citizen of New York. . . ." The countless evils which lurk in the dark corners of our civic institutions, which stalk abroad in the slums, and have their permanent abode in the crowded tenement houses, have met in Mr. Riis the most formidable opponent . . . to Mr. Riis was given, in addition to earnestness and zeal, the great gift of expression, the great gift of mak-

ing others see what he saw and feel what he felt....

For his part, Riis stumped ardently for Roosevelt and wrote a laudatory campaign biography. ("It is strenuous," said a critic. "It is loud, it is fervent.... It is hoarsely enthusiastic, and it is all pitched in one high monotonous key of laudation.") Riis never publicly differed with his friend, except in the most roundabout way. On one occasion he told an audience: "... permit me to say it, that your great and splendid city has been ... pauperized in its citizenship by great wealth and perilous prosperity.... However, this is politics, which I shall not discuss. The President of the United States says that my opinion in that quarter is no good at all, and you are free to adopt his view. I will endorse his views — most of the time — anywhere."

Though Riis was most often associated with the battle against the slums, he helped bring about reform in many areas — child labor laws, playgrounds for schools, establishment of small neighborhood parks. One of his most important pieces of investigative reporting may have saved thousands of New York residents from the scourge of cholera—an exposé of the city's contaminated water supply. The story appeared in the *Evening Sun* August 21, 1891, under the headline SOME THINGS WE DRINK. With the story were six of his photographs, which apparently later vanished into the files of the newspaper. "I took my camera and went up in the watershed photographing my evidence wherever I found it. Populous towns sewered directly into our drinking water. I went to the doctors and asked how many days a vigorous cholera bacillus may live and multiply in running water. About seven, said they. My case was made." His words and pictures led to the purchase of the extensive Croton Watershed.

Many of Riis's stories were controversial, even among progressives sympathetic to his crusades. Himself an immigrant, he occasionally spoke out against unrestricted immigration. He knew that the tenements to which the newcomers flocked already were dangerously overcrowded and that every new boatload of cheap labor further depressed wage scales in the city's sweatshops. (In sharp contrast to Riis's practical viewpoint was the brazen bigotry of the man known as "the father of American photography," Samuel F. B. Morse, the portrait painter and inventor of the telegraph. Morse wanted to deny U.S. citizenship to all new immigrants, whom he labeled "priest-ridden slaves of Ireland and Germany" and "outcast tenants of the poor houses and prisons of Europe.")

Riis justifiably could be chided for his occasional exaggerated characterization of some groups in the polyglot population of New York. Some of his remarks have disturbed those of us who have lent their voices in protest against the use of racial and ethnic stereotypes by public figures. My own faith in racial brotherhood was set forth in a book that I co-authored in 1945, *The Springfield Plan.* It was based on the biblical injunction "Thou shalt love thy neighbor as thyself" and that, if America is to endure as a free and united country, the many races and faiths that make America must live together in mutual respect. The racist senator from Mississippi, Theodore Bilbo, so detested the book that soon after its publication he said its supporters "should be totally ostracized from decent, right-thinking and right-living white people in every community in America." In Jacob Riis's case, I am sure he wrote without malice. He had to develop a folksy style using the jargon of the lower depths where he worked. Because of his down-to-earth approach, he was read and listened to in greater degree than any of his more sophisticated colleagues. "I had no stomach for abstract discussions," he said. "I wanted to right those of them that I could reach."

Throughout the 1890's Riis continued his newspaper and magazine broadsides. His pen was the incisive edge of a growing reform movement that had been augmented by young enthusiasts who flocked to the settlement houses and other progressive new groups and institutions. Riis's stubbornly enduring single-mindedness served them as an example. Before Riis took up the cudgel, most New York reform efforts tended to ebb and flow. In the 1870's, Frank Leslie's *Illustrated Newspaper* described a lecture meeting about poverty: "The lecture was delivered to a room full of people, who listened, sympathized and went away — doing nothing." To those who got discouraged at the length of the battle, Riis would counsel patience and remind them of "the Israelites that marched seven times around Jericho and blew their horns before the walls fell."

His battle to raze the dreadful slums around the Five Points area to replace them with a park took fourteen years. His exposés helped spark the Drexel Committee Investigation of ramshackle firetrap tenements, which existed in defiance of laws relating to light, air and sanitary requirements. Riis himself sat in on the investigation and learned many of the techniques that enabled him to dig out facts for his reporting. The investigation resulted in the Small Park Act of 1887, but it took nine more years of boat-rocking by Riis and others before the infamous Mulberry Bend was replaced by a park.

The formal opening of the park was held on June 15, 1897. Riis wasn't even invited to the ceremonies, though he was formally entitled to an invitation as secretary of the Small Parks Committee, a citizens' group. He went anyway, accompanied by his fellow muckraker Lincoln Steffens. They were pleased to find thousands of boys and girls eagerly waiting for the ceremonies to start. A band played. There were speeches by the mayor and lesser dignitaries — some of whom had for years opposed the efforts of the Small Parks Committee. The final speaker was the street-cleaning commissioner, who placed credit for the park where it belonged and called for three cheers for Jacob Riis. The crowd roared, "Hooray, Jacob Riis!" Other such parks were created and Riis came to be known as "the father of the small parks movement."

New reform agencies sprang up — among them the Citizens Union and the Social Reform Club. Riis's tenacious reporting and superhuman optimism set their model of good citizenship. "Have we not all seen it? Have we not seen the boss dethroned, graft and iniquity exposed, the muckrake plied until the stench of it was sickening? Yet let us be comforted. The muck has to be raked up before it can be carted away, and the devil is not cast out without a prodigious noise. He is wedged in the doorway now, but he is going out, and that soon. It is good to live in this strenuous day that took him by the throat."

Chapter 6

Evangelist for Reform

One of the happiest and most fulfilling years in Jacob Riis's life was 1901. He and Elizabeth celebrated their silver wedding anniversary; their good friend Theodore Roosevelt became President; Tammany Hall's hold on New York City was broken by the forces of reform; his highly successful autobiography was published; and finally he felt secure enough as a writer and lecturer to give up his daily job as a newspaper reporter.

Even as his income from lectures and books grew, Riis still had to struggle to make ends meet. The family now numbered five children — Edward, Clara, John, Kate and Roger William, plus his first grandchild — and only after fifteen years of arduous effort had he managed to pay off the mortgage on their Long Island home. When friend Lincoln Steffens told him he didn't charge enough for his lectures, Riis only shrugged and turned away. As the following entry from one of his account books shows, he tended to count his blessings as well as the money. "Took in $3450.60 in 1895. Gosh what a lot of money. Where did it all go to? I am . . . earning as much as I ever will, with nothing going in the bank for a rainy day. . . . Let us see what I have against it: a good wife, the best that ever lived, good children, none of whom will ever be rich, but all of whom I hope and believe, will be always good, standing up for the right and fight for it if need be. A place of usefulness for myself, friends, good and true — what more can a man want?"

Riis's autobiography *The Making of an American* sold out two editions in three weeks. It was the ideal saga of an immigrant boy who had made good. What's more, it told in detail the story of the rich girl he had lost and then regained, including a chapter by Elizabeth herself on their long courtship. One critic attacked Riis's "little regard for dignity or domestic privacy," but readers loved the romance of the book and Elizabeth became a kind of national figure in her own right. By August 1902 Riis had yet another book out, *The Battle with the Slum*, which was dedicated to Theodore Roosevelt as a record of the battles they waged together. The book contained much material that Riis already had published in magazines — slum life, the inadequacies of schools and playgrounds, exploitation of little children who worked at home, the slave labor system in the sweatshops. The book also carried his reminiscenses of the wretched alleyways, the notorious landmarks of human degradation now long gone — Battle Alley, Kerosene Row, Poverty Gap, Bandit's Roost, Thieves' Alley, Hell's Kitchen, Cat Alley. "It thrills you as much as the most exciting romance," said one critic, "and for far better purpose. Its brief, crackling sentences tell of the noblest most high minded, most desperate fight ever waged — that for decency, cleanliness, and a chance to breathe and live like a man."

There were now seven books by Riis, some in several editions. They were on the lists of recommended reading in schools and libraries, and their homespun philosophy was often quoted by sociologists and reformers. Riis's observations may seem commonplace today, but they were radical in his time. Some examples:

The tenement is a destroyer of home and character, of the individuality that makes character tell. A homeless city – a city without civic pride, without citizen virtue is a despoiler of children, a de-

stroyer of the tomorrow.

You cannot make a good citizen out of the lad whom you denied a chance to kick a ball across lots when that was his ambition and his right; it takes a whole boy to make a whole man.

A man cannot be expected to live like a pig and vote like a man.

The very enforcement of law has sometimes seemed a travesty: the boy who steals fifty cents is sent to the House of Correction; the man who steals a railroad goes free.

The bad environment becomes the heredity of the next generation, given the crowd, you have the slum ready-made.

There is needed only the strong and informed public opinion that sees clearly the peril, to set a barrier against the inroads of the slum. Without that we fight in vain.

Our country has grown great – our cities wealthy – but in their slums lurk poverty and bitterness – bitterness because the promise has not been kept that every man should have an even chance to start with.

The poor we shall have always with us, but the slum we need not have. These two do not rightfully belong together. Their present partnership is at once poverty's worst hardship and our worst blunder.

Every baby is entitled to one pair of mother's arms.

By the early 1900's the writings of Riis, Steffens and the other muckrakers had popularized the subject of social reform. New national organizations sprang forth to serve as clearinghouses for reform projects of every kind. At a gathering of the National Conference of Charities and Corrections, representatives from all over the country came to give testimony about the many movements under way. Civic leaders everywhere regarded Riis as an expert who could give them encouragement and point the way to enactment of practical reforms in their cities and towns. So Riis left his familiar slum battleground in New York and became a nationwide evangelist for reform. He had learned on one of his early ventures out of the city that his crusade was needed everywhere. "Standing . . . on a mountainside in New Hampshire with a matchless view stretched out before me, I said to my friend, the good rector . . . Here everybody must surely be good. How can they help it? He looked at me sadly and said, pointing to the scattered farms lying so peacefully in the landscape: 'If you could go with me into those homes and see the things I see in many of them you would quit your Mulberry Bend and transfer your battle with the slum to our hillside!' "

Each of Riis's two main activities were of twenty-five years' duration. He became a full-fledged reporter in 1876 and gave it up in 1901. He started to lecture in 1888 and continued through 1913. "Now my winters are spent on the lecture platform altogether," he wrote after leaving newspaper work. "I always liked the work. It tires less than the office routine and you feel the touch with fellows more than when you sit and write your message."

At the height of his popularity Riis kept three lecture bureaus busy. His engagements sometimes brought him as much as $150 per lecture, though part of the proceeds went for transportation and lodging. All would have been well but for his failing health. For some time he had experienced painful attacks, which he attributed to indigestion brought on by hastily swallowed meals. He finally consulted a doctor who found a serious heart condition, angina pectoris. In an epilogue for a new edition of *The Making of an American,* Riis's grandson, Dr. J. Riis Owre, described the intensity of his grandfather's lecture schedule: "The first of his long lecture tours began in January 1902. It took him from East to the Middle West and back again to New England. According to his pocket diary for 1902, some seventy lectures were scheduled in the period from Jan. 2 to April 11 — a rigorous schedule for one who had had a major heart attack only two years earlier."

Despite his poor health and advancing years — he was now in his fifties — Riis liked the lecture circuit. The warmth of his audiences made him optimistic about the future of reform. In an article entitled "Experiences of Popular Lecturer," he related some causes for optimism:

I was to lecture at Cedar Falls and was laid up at a Junction, waiting for my train. At the lunchtable were three typical Iowa farmers, all bound for the lecture. They are great people. I have known them to travel forty miles across the frozen prairie to hear a lecturer in whom they were interested. In that same winter I spoke in a little town a dozen miles beyond the bluffs of the Mississippi River, where the population, men, women, and children, numbered three hundred. To my amazed inquiry of where the audience was to come from, the manager of the lecture said simply, "You wait." And when at night I found the hall jammed with a crowd that numbered at least six hundred, he took me to the window and pointed to a great host of teams and wagons below. Some of them had come from the next county. I have sometimes wondered how they got home. When I started at four in the morning a sleet-storm was raging, with the snow lying foot-deep. . . . I go across the country in the course of the. winter sometimes twice. And I record without hesitation my conviction that we are very much awake. The evidence is, on every hand, that the people are thinking. . . . Every day it is brought home to us that we "belong," that as people we have to solve our problems together since apart we never can. . . . Compare that, now, with the day that was, when we in my city stood by unprotesting while a church that had grown wealthy moved uptown from Mulberry Street, trading off its House of God to the devil in human shape of conscienceless builders who cut it up into rooms and filled it with tenants who in their cubbyholes knew neither light nor air and died like flies. . . . I have struggled with the Mulberry Bend and seen it go down . . . all about me I see the dawn breaking. Are we gaining?

Here, yesterday, came a letter asking me to come to Scranton, where they are getting ready to give the children playgrounds. They wanted me to help. . . . Do you wonder that I think we are gaining?

Riis did not have to vary his lectures greatly since his audiences were widely scattered around the country. He banged away at the same basic stories, as he did in his writing, building on true stories from his personal experience. One of his favorite subjects was the "Battle with the Slum" of the 1880's and 90's, the struggle that resulted in the passage of many reforms. He would preface the show of his lantern slides with these prophetic words: "Think not that any of them are irrelevant because of things that were. Those things are but shadows of what may come again, if we lose our grip and once more let our conscience fall asleep, believing that we have done so much that all is well." Another lecture was "Tony," the story of a boy of the streets who needed help if he was to grow up as a useful member of society. His words described the suffering of the poor; his photographs, blown up large on the projection screen, brought home the reality of it.

In January 1905 Riis took time out from his lectures to attend the second inauguration of his friend Teddy Roosevelt. Elizabeth and the children were already in Washington waiting for him, and it was a big day for all of them. Riis felt a sense of personal triumph — he had campaigned for Roosevelt and his biography of the President had sold widely and contributed to his friend's victory. In March he left home again for a two-month lecture tour. This time he went on the road reluctantly; Elizabeth had been ill for several weeks and he was worried. He was nearing the end of the tour when the urgent telegram reached him. He hurried home to find the entire family assembled: Kate and young Roger William who lived at home, Clara from her nearby home, Edward from California, John from Colorado. Riis's diary tells the story: "May 5 — Dr. Jewett came. Said lungs involved. May 6 — Dr. . . . said Bronchial-Pneumonia.

May 18 — Lammeth died. God help us all." "Lammeth" means little lamb in Danish; it was the nickname he had given to Elizabeth on their first Christmas together when, to cheer up his homesick wife, he had brought her a picture of the Good Shepherd protecting his flock. The tenderness of the scene had made him think of her, and from that day on he had called her by no other name. Elizabeth was buried at Maple Grove Cemetery, in sight of their home.

Newspapers across the country carried long obituaries and from the White House came a telegram: BELOVED FRIEND: IN THE TERRIBLE ELEMENTAL GRIEF NO ONE, NO MATTER HOW CLOSE, CAN GIVE ANY REAL COMFORT. . . . YOU KNOW HOW MY WIFE AND I LOVED THE DEAR, DEAR ONE WHO HAS GONE BEFORE YOU; YOU KNOW HOW WE LOVE YOU, HOW WE THINK OF YOU, HOW WE FEEL FOR YOU IN YOUR CRUSHING CALAMITY. THE LIFE OF YOU TWO WAS AN IDEAL LIFE. . . .

Riis was overcome by grief. "I can hardly weep any more," he wrote to a friend. "But in the still of night-watches the loneliness of it all comes upon me and it is dreadful. Still I shall try to take up a man's work and do it, and so it may be that the road shall not seem so long or so hard anymore. . . ." Two months after her death, Riis took up his work. He wrote a magazine article, spoke at memorial services for a friend and resumed a heavy lecture schedule. Nothing could break him, but the next two years were an ordeal of constant travel and deep loneliness. Other things went wrong. His older children were not doing well and depended on him for support. The two youngest were boarded out and needed care and planned education. Expenses mounted and, because of his failing health, he worried more than ever about money. The house in Richmond Hill was rented: the family scattered.

Chapter 7

The Last Years

In the spring of 1907 Riis broke the news of his plans to remarry. To his son John he wrote: ". . . the nest is empty, and I am a lonely homeless man. . . . Miss Phillips is thirty, and she is a woman who has seen much of life. Like myself, she longs for a home. . . . Sometime in late summer we will quietly marry." And to his younger daughter: ". . . I too have to begin over again, and it is well so, for a man may not lay down his work and still live. . . . I shall do my best, and be glad for the old home and for a voice at the gate to hail my coming."

Mary Phillips was twenty-eight years younger than Riis, a St. Louis society girl who had heard one of his lectures and been greatly impressed by his sincerity and dedication. She became his secretary and, during his time of grief, an energetic and cheerful companion. A native of Memphis, she grew up in St. Louis where her father was president of the cotton exchange. She finished her education in England and France and had a short stint as an actress in New York. Riis considered himself fortunate to have merited a woman so much younger than he. There is a letter that he wrote to her five months after Elizabeth's death addressed "Dearest girl" and signed with an informality unusual for Riis: "So long, sweet — your old Jake."

Dr. Owre speaks warmly of his step-grandmother: ". . . she had a rare and beautiful zest for living; there were few things that did not arouse her curiosity. . . ." She and Riis had waited a year and a half before deciding to marry, and Dr. Owre indicates she must have had reservations even then. She told Dr. Owre in 1964: "I really did not love your grandfather, when I married him. I admired him enor-

mously. I was fascinated by him. He was the most exciting man I had ever met, but I did not love him. It was not until several months later, when I went to meet him on one of his lecture tours, that I realized I really loved him." Dr. Owre notes that Riis's second marriage was thus not unlike his first: "Devotion and admiration and respect and loneliness . . . were to turn into mutual love — adoration even — and what followed was to be an idyll." (Many years later Mary Riis made refreshingly clear that her husband was no saint: "I've heard a little swearing, of course, but nothing to compare with Jake, the first time I heard his anger aroused. His swearing simply swept me off my feet.")

After a brief honeymoon late in the summer, Riis brought his bride to Richmond Hill and the old home was opened again. Under Mary, the home's Danish atmosphere gradually became distinctly American, but its friendliness and courtesy did not change. Once again it was a house open to Riis's friends and a refuge where he could write and relax. His youngest son Roger William — known as "Vivi" — had a home to come to from boarding school. Mary took to the boy immediately, an affection that developed into a lifelong friendship. Riis himself went at his work with renewed zeal. He planned another book and a trip to Europe, wrote magazine articles and resumed his lectures. Thanks to his wide-ranging lecture tours, he now wrote knowledgeably about the entire country. In 1908 his articles included "Heading off the Slums in the West," "How Helena Became a City," "Playgrounds in Washington and Elsewhere" and "The Plight of St. Louis."

The contrasting roles played by Riis's two wives are revealed in a letter he wrote to his sister. Of Elizabeth he wrote: "She made me all that I am. It isn't much, but it is her work. . . . There was always something sacred about her to me. . . ." Of Mary: ". . . of an entirely different sphere than myself — but I saw the genuine true soul in her, and I was not mistaken." He made special note of her acute business sense: "I have always written my stories and let them pay what they thought them worth. Mary told me they did not pay enough. That never occurred to me. At her request I notified them all to pay me hereafter 5 cents a word. They yelled yes! and just begged me to write. But heretofore everybody paid me 1½ or 2 cents a word."

In the summer of 1908 Jacob and Mary went to Germany, taking young Roger William with them. Riis's heart had been giving him trouble, and they hoped that the famous baths at Nauheim would help him. From Germany they went to his hometown Ribe, where Mary met his relatives and friends. While in Ribe, Riis gathered research for a book about the town and his own youth. Back home, rested and feeling better, he finished the book by late fall and it was published the following year as *The Old Town*. The illustrations in the book were freely drawn, unlike several previous Riis books, which carried line drawings or halftones from his photographs. The drawings were by Vladyslaw T. Benda, a well-known American artist. The antiquarian at the Museum of Ribe, Mogens Bencard, noted that the drawings were a "mixture of free version of old photographs and Riis' and Benda's combined imagination."

Mary Riis, pleased that the trip abroad had reinvigorated her husband, encouraged him to write more about his native land. He decided to undertake a volume of short biographies of some Danish heroes. The project, quite different from his previous writing based on personal experience, required researching old records that could be found only in Copenhagen. In the summer of 1910 they sailed for Denmark. They again visited Ribe, where the entire town gave them a very warm reception, and the baths at Nauheim. The trip home was leisurely and took them through Switzerland and Italy, with short stopovers in Greece, Algiers and Spain.

Riis felt better, but he continued to fret about finances. When he remarried, Mary had insisted he put his savings in trust for his children. She did not want to be the beneficiary of his years of hard work and self-denial. Now, wrote Dr. Owre, "he knew his earning years were limited and every cent thus expended diminished the provision he wanted to make for his wife. It was a problem that was to be with him to the end of his days — one of those unhappy mixtures of economics and personality for which there was no solution."

The family's decision to move to the country added to the financial worries. Richmond Hill was no longer the open, quiet country that they wanted. In Barre, Massachusetts, they found and bought Pine Brook Acres, a hundred-year-old house and two hundred acres, and set about restoring both house and land. "The next May," Dr. Owre wrote, "Mary and Jake established themselves there, in a tent while the house was being renovated and for the summer only, since there was no furnace. It was an adventure, a new experience, for both. Mary was the farmer. She pored over textbooks, planted twenty acres of potatoes, planted apple trees, picked potato bugs, bossed farm hands, began to recondition the soil by raising clover and rye and vetch and plowing them under."

Restoration of the farm was expensive and Riis would not slacken his lecture pace. In the late summer of 1912 he interrupted his lecture tour to stump for Teddy Roosevelt, who hoped his party would nominate him for a second full term in the White House. Riis's diary shows that, from September 16 to October 24, he spoke in fifteen cities for Roosevelt — often three and four times a day. Now past sixty, he found the lecture trips more and more tiring. He was dissatisfied with the bookings provided by his agents: they were too few and too many miles apart. In the early fall, in a letter to his daughter, Riis appeared resigned to slowing down: "My heart is very much enlarged and has only a small margin to run on. . . . I expect henceforth to limit my activities and, as far as possible, to let my lecturing go. It is too bad — a couple of years more would have put our farm on a paying basis so that we might live off, and on it. . . ."

Riis fulfilled his current lecture engagement, then returned to the sanitarium in Battle Creek, Michigan, where he had previously gone for a rest. In November he went on a short speaking tour, a trip eased by the companionship of his wife. Toward Christmas they returned to New York and rented an apartment. He felt well enough in early December to cover for three New York newspapers the proceedings of the National House Conference in Philadelphia. He also wrote an article for *The Century* under the old familiar title "The Battle with the Slum." The article acknowledged the gains made in the past twenty-five years but appealed for an intensified fight against sweatshops and the elimination of bad housing conditions, which were conducive to the spread of tuberculosis. Riis was particularly concerned about that dread disease; it had claimed the lives of six of his brothers. Christmas in New York was an unusually cheerful one. He loved the holiday season, wrote many stories about it and originated several new American Christmas traditions, including the idea of Christmas seals for the benefit of tuberculosis research. This holiday season he and Mary attended a Riis-inspired New York ritual — the huge New Year's celebration in Madison Square where 100,000 gathered to sing songs that were projected onto enormous screens with stereopticons.

The following spring Riis completed another lecture tour, then spent the summer at Pine Brook Farm. Mary's mother had come to live with them. Roger William was home from college. Riis's other children made frequent visits. In December he wrote to his sister: "Yes, I am well again and I have been out lecturing. But you are right. I cannot do it the way I could before and the risk is really too great. On the last journey I caught a terrible cold. Had that turned into pneumonia it would have been over with my heart. But it is, of course, my livelihood." He went again to the sanitarium in Battle Creek, then took up his lecture tour to Chicago, and south through Texas and Louisiana. In New Orleans he collapsed and hurried back to Battle Creek, where he came down with bronchitis. Mary's last letter to her husband begged him to discontinue the tour and come home: "Billy and I have had a long talk about money, and we both feel that you must give up this lecturing entirely. We will slowly build up a good farm business and a preserve business and in a few years we will be really well off. Don't ever think that you are a burden to me, heart of my heart, you are my reason for living, my joy of life."

Early in May, she received urgent word from her husband in the sanitarium. Though spent with his illness, he wanted to come home. She and Roger William rushed to Battle Creek to bring him back. "The railroad journey was almost more than his strength could endure," wrote Dr. Owre. "Then came the automobile trip, over a rough road. Just before they came in sight of the farm, Riis collapsed again. He rallied briefly, and then began to lose strength each day. Friends gathered and messages of sympathy poured in. Riis fell into a coma; occasionally he was able to recognize those around him. On May 26, 1914, he died . . . he was . . . buried, as he had specified, under an unmarked granite boulder in the cemetery situated down the hill from the farm."

Chapter 8

An Epilogue

Long before his death, Jacob Riis had ended his career as photographer. There is no evidence that he made pictures for his own use after 1898. He had prepared a sufficient number of lantern slides for his lectures; by his pragmatic standards, he had no further need for the new craft he had taught himself. On his visits to Ribe he purchased pictures of whatever Danish scenes he required for lectures and books. In his ledger there are entries for two such purchases. He apparently did not make family snapshots. I asked Dr. Owre about his grandfather's photographic activities and received the following reply: "I don't remember my mother or my aunts and uncles talking of their father as a photographer. . . . In his letters — I have read most of them — he never mentions a camera. He bought post cards of scenes he liked. I remember when he visited us in Minneapolis in 1912, and I am sure I should have remembered him taking pictures if he had done so."

While his photography was quickly forgotten, Riis's voluminous writings and other papers took their place in major libraries and archives, including the Library of Congress. In addition to his letters and diaries, there were fifteen books, more than one hundred magazine articles and at least two hundred major newspaper feature stories — plus the countless newspaper reports that were unsigned and difficult to attribute to him. As the years went by, even the reputation of Riis the writer and reformer became obscured by the worldwide tumult of events. By modern times his name was scarcely known, except for a park and a settlement house in New York and a boulder with a plaque in Riis Park in Chicago bearing the name Jacob Riis.

I first became interested in Riis in 1941 when a book critic compared my own work to that of the great muckraker. I knew that there were certain similarities in our lives — both of us were immigrants, both of us were involved in social reform. In a secondhand bookstore I found Riis's autobiography and discovered that we had something else in common. I came to the page where Riis described how he learned about taking pictures by flashlight and became a photographer. The next morning I rushed to the bookstores along the Bowery, where Riis had spent many of his newspaper days. Among the half-dozen Riis books I found — all of them long out of print — was *How the Other Half Lives*. The title page bore the confirmation I sought: "With illustrations chiefly from photographs taken by the author."

Though a documentary photographer for many years and a teacher of the subject, I had not heretofore learned of Riis's photography. Nor had I seen old photographs that could compare with the simple, powerful immediacy of those in his books. Seeking Riis photographs, I went to the Museum of the City of New York, the New York Historical Society, the New York Public Library, city and social agencies and finally the Jacob A. Riis Neighborhood Settlement House. I could not find a single Riis photograph; I could not find anyone who knew anything about his photography. My search widened. I inquired of the Library of Congress, the Smithsonian, the George Eastman Museum of Photography. I contacted photo agencies, newspaper morgues, manufacturers of lantern slides. I checked books and magazines devoted to photography during the years from 1880 to 1900. Not one mentioned Riis.

Finally, in January 1942, I located Jacob Riis's second wife Mary and sent her a letter. To identify myself, I noted that I was the photo editor of *Common Ground,* the publication of the Common Council for American Unity, of which she was a member of the board of directors. I told her that I was most eager to bring to light her husband's photography and asked if she had his negatives. When no reply came, I telephoned Mrs. Riis at her office in a Wall Street brokerage firm. She said she was too busy to talk then. After months of unsuccessful attempts to discuss the matter with her by phone, I was referred by Mrs. Riis to her stepson Roger William Riis. I had a long talk with Roger William at his Fifth Avenue public relations office. He agreed that his father's pictures ought to be found and put to some use, but said he had no idea where they were and doubted they could be found. I sensed that he wondered why I was so interested. At any rate, he promised to see what he could find. Later I learned that the Riis family had been rather careless with memorabilia: among the first editions that I picked up in secondhand bookshops was a copy of *The Old Town* inscribed to the eldest son, "Edward Riis, affectionately, from his father, Jacob A. Riis."

Over the next few years I kept up my search for the Riis negatives. I rummaged without success through antique and junk shops, finding in the process a number of other old glass-plate negatives that enriched my own collection of early photographs. The war was on and I went off on frequent assignments to take photographs for military training manuals. I also completed my book *American Counterpoint,* a photographic study of American ethnic groups, and began discussions for an exhibition of the original prints at the Museum of the City of New York.

I stayed in touch with Roger William Riis, but there was no new information. He was always very gracious and kept my hopes up. In 1945 I went to see him again. Together we reconstructed Jacob Riis's whereabouts shortly before his death and concluded that the negatives and lantern slides must have been left on the farm in Massachusetts. I suggested Roger William should visit Pine Brook Farm to search the attic where some of his father's personal effects were stored after the funeral.

At this point, my frustration was mounting. The many years of procrastination by the Riis family led me to resort to a slightly devious strategy. I suggested to Miss Grace Mayer, a curator at the Museum of the City of New York, that she write Riis saying that the museum was trying to locate his father's pictures. A month later Riis brought to the museum a box containing 163 lantern slides which had been found at the farm. I was delighted to see the old pictures in any form and began work in the darkroom. Lantern slides are positive images; they must be converted into negatives from which prints can be reproduced. Many of the slides were cracked, faded or discolored. These had to be enlarged into paper negatives and turned into positives through contact printing so that the damage could be retouched. Only then could they be photographed as negatives and the final prints made. After several months of tedious work I had a portfolio of satisfactory prints. I rushed them to the office of *U.S. Camera,* certain that the editors would want to break the news of my discovery in their 1947 Annual. Two months later I received an apologetic note saying, "Although the story is good, the decision is, unfortunately, in the negative."

I was perplexed but decided to prepare a brief monograph that would include Riis's photographs, a condensed biography and the story of discovering his work. I asked my secretary to type the manuscript without making copies. Alas, the young lady was more disposed to helping a friend than being loyal to her employer. It soon came to my attention that a popular photographic magazine had accepted a feature on Jacob Riis and scheduled it for publication. The author had thinly disguised what I had written and added a number of paragraphs from Riis's own writings. As it turned out, publication of his piece was delayed and was not the first account of Riis's photography to appear.

Then occurred the event that made worthwhile my nearly five years of searching, prodding and hoping. Some time before, I had suggested to Roger William Riis that he look for the negatives in the old family house in Richmond Hill on Long Island. He promised to alert the occupants. A few months later the house was sold and about to be torn down. The owners, rummaging around the attic, found stored between the rafters the priceless photographs of Jacob Riis — 412 glass negatives, 161 lantern slides and 193 prints. They took the collection to Roger William's home in Manhattan and, finding no one there, left it outside the door.

On November 15, 1946, R. W. Riis presented the collection to the Museum of the City of New York. Now the road was open for presenting his father's photography to the world. Miss Mayer, curator of prints, and I decided an exhibit of his prints should open the following May, the month of Riis's birth. I selected fifty negatives I considered to be most representative of his work and began preparing prints. At first I was dismayed when I saw the original negatives. In his haste to bring before the public the evidence contained in his negatives, Riis had neglected to fix and wash them properly and some had deteriorated. The negatives presented an even more serious problem, which required a carefully controlled method of printing. In Riis's day, photographic emulsion was not as sensitive to all colors as it is in modern film. It did not reproduce tonal values correctly and, as a result, parts of the negatives were either overexposed or underexposed, thus creating unnatural contrast. If an old glass negative is held up to the light, the image is seen in full detail because our eyes concentrate on the darker areas while skimming over the lighter ones. In printing from such negatives, however, an even exposure does not render the gradation of tones from black to white in the same relationship as they appear to the eye. Riis could not possibly have visualized precisely the entire gamut of values that would appear in the final prints. He was totally unaware of the "interrelation of the three principal variables — subject brightness, exposure and development"—and I don't think he was much concerned about technical perfection in his photographs. In making lantern slides, Alfred Stieglitz worked out ingenious chemical techniques for controlling contrast and tone and a means of expanding the range of values by the use of a mask. In printing Riis's negatives, I similarly controlled the exposure by masking out various parts.

Meanwhile, my search for additional historical material to enhance the show led me to a trunk filled with Riis manuscripts and letters at the New York Public Library. I first heard about the trunk from Mitchell Kennerley, a pioneer in publishing and exhibiting photographs. He told me the first of three dramatically different versions of how the trunk had come to the library. His story had it that agents of the library had snatched the manuscripts and letters from the Massachusetts farm while Riis's family were still at his funeral. Another version came from Riis's grandson Dr. Owre, who heard it from the former chief of the library's research section. This man told him that many years ago, hearing that tenants of the farm were using Riis's papers to light fires, he had sent agents to rescue the papers. The third version was related to me by Paul R. Rugen, the library's keeper of manuscripts. According to Rugen, the library had learned of the papers in 1936 from Jacob Riis Praeger, president of the Jacob A. Riis Youth Foundation in Boston. "The farm at Barre was owned (not rented)," said Rugen, "and the story of 'using the Riis papers to light fires' would appear to be apocryphal."

The show was announced as "Special Exhibition, 'The Battle With the Slum,' 1887–1897. Fifty Prints by Alexander Alland from the original negatives by Jacob A. Riis, presented to the Museum by Roger William Riis. May 20 through September 14, 1947." In her introduction for the show Miss Mayer wrote:

About 5 years ago Alexander Alland – himself engaged in the battle for which Jacob A. Riis gave his life – made a discovery that eventu-

ally led to the present exhibition. Searching for early pictorial records of the lives of newcomers to America's shore, he came upon a group of illustrations by Jacob A. Riis that antedated all others. Searching further, he established the fact that Jacob A. Riis was the first journalist photographer to make use of the flashlight to document the social scene. Through Alexander Alland's efforts the monumental Riis Collection was rediscovered and generously given to the Museum by Roger William Riis. As a labor of love, Alexander Alland has made the fifty exhibition prints from the fading 4 × 5 glass negatives, brilliantly surmounting the most difficult technical problems to bring back these epic documents of the eighties and nineties to fight again "The Battle With the Slum."

Much credit for the show must go to Miss Mayer, whose labors far exceeded her normal duties as a curator. She did painstaking research for the preparation of captions, the introduction and publicity for the show. For text that appeared with each picture, she extracted lengthy passages from Riis's copious writing. This approach made each photograph an independent unit, which then reinforced the other photographs so as to create an intensely fascinating narrative.

From the start the show was one of the most popular ever held at the museum. It was not dismantled until January 1948, long beyond the scheduled closing date. Beaumont Newhall said in his *History of Photography:* "The photographs are direct and penetrating, as raw as the sordid scenes which they so often represent. Riis chose unerringly the camera stand which would most effectively tell the story." Newhall commented to me when he first saw the prints: "I was bowled over by the Riis prints . . . Miss Mayer showed me some of the original negatives, and I could quickly see that you have done wonders with them." The 1948 *U.S. Camera Annual*, which devoted ten pages to the Riis pictures, called them "one of the greatest sets of documentary pictures in American photographic history."

I wanted the whole world to know about the pictures. Years of research had convinced me that most of the ma-

terial in museums is relegated to oblivion and seen by few. I did not want this to happen to Riis. I knew that he would have wanted his pictures used by reform forces in furtherance of his lifelong crusade. I outlined my intentions to Roger William Riis — traveling shows, magazine articles, lectures, a book — and he acknowledged approval. At the outset of our association he had written to me: ". . . anything you wish to do with my father's pictures and slides, is entirely agreeable to me. . . ."

To expedite wide distribution of Riis's photographs here and abroad, I engaged a reputable photo agency. Within a few months, features on Riis were accepted by publications in Holland, Sweden and America. Then came an unexpected snag. The editors of *Harper's Bazaar* questioned my agent's right to sell Riis's photos in view of the fact that the same pictures were being released by the museum free of charge. The museum had assured me that Riis's negatives would be given out only to me, and I had taken it for granted that all requests for his photographs would be referred to me. I conveyed to Roger William Riis my fears that indiscriminate release of the photographs by the museum might jeopardize their meaningful use. He responded immediately with a request to the museum: ". . . as to the use of my father's negatives or photos . . . I think there should be one condition, in justice to Mr. Alland, and the marked service he has performed on his own initiative and at his own expense: I believe that when the Museum receives a request for use of those negatives or photos from a profitmaking concern, such as a magazine or newspaper, the request should go through Mr. Alland . . . he ought to have a chance to recoup a little, at least, in exchange for his great services to history and to the city."

My attempts to preserve the Riis photographic heritage in other museums ran into difficulties at first. New York's Metropolitan Museum of Art and the Museum of Modern Art both offered thanks and regrets. I was more successful at the New York Historical Society, which now has some 150

Riis prints I made from the original negatives, along with several hundred prints made from my own collection of historical glass plates by other early photographers. The lack of foresight shown by some museums was not greatly surprising to me. Too often such institutions as the Library of Congress ask that photographers and artists bequeath them important documents and artifacts. This practice is unfair and undignified and does not ensure a flow of valuable materials into our national museums and archives. What is needed is a U.S. Department of Antiquity; until that day, Congress should earmark annual monies for acquiring historical material. As it stands now, many treasures are in danger of being lost. Once, I was present in the office of a museum when someone telephoned to offer for sale a photographic collection found in the attic of an old Dutch colonial house. The caller was advised that the museum did not have funds for such purchases but did accept gifts. I spoke to the caller and acquired, for a token payment, the work of a very skilled photographer, the one-time secretary of Stieglitz's New York Camera Club.

Even the Museum of the City of New York, home of the Riis Collection, failed to give full and proper acknowledgment of the manner in which the photographs were saved. In the fall of 1973 I wrote to the director, Joseph Veach Noble: "I am proud that I have made a noteworthy contribution to the preservation of our Nation's and the City of New York's historical heritage, and I think that the users of Riis' pictures should also be aware of it. . . ." He responded by awarding me the museum's commemorative medal and acknowledging "a debt to you which the Museum can never adequately repay." Writing of the museum's "expanding years" 1932 – 1959, Albert K. Baragwanath, senior curator, noted that among the great treasures of New York history that came to the museum during these years were Eugene O'Neill's manuscripts, a complete room with Duncan Phyfe furniture, a man's suit worn to Washington's Inaugural Ball, and the negatives taken by Jacob Riis. (The question of the museum's right to the Riis Collection was raised by Riis's wife long before her death at the age of ninety. Nothing came of her letter to the museum, though the man who was then director was prepared to battle it out in the courts if she brought suit. Mrs. Riis received no remuneration for the use of her husband's pictures.)

The rediscovery of Riis's photographs sparked a long resurgence of interest in the great reformer. The Riis Collection, one of the most popular in America, has averaged nearly five hundred print requests a year for the past twenty years — for books, exhibitions, films and classrooms. They are used here and abroad to promote the cause of human decency. In Denmark an exhibition of his pictures—including the showing of a film in which Dr. Owre and I participated — toured some thirty-five cities. Riis's old Richmond Hill home was designated a National Historic Landmark in 1971 by the U.S. Department of Interior — through the efforts of Felix J. Cuervo, president of the Native New Yorkers Historical Association. A commemorative plaque was purchased with contributions from schoolchildren, but when the owner of the house refused to cooperate Mr. Cuervo had to nail the plaque to a tree. The plaque was lost when municipal workers trimmed the tree. Two years after being declared a landmark, the house was razed to make way for new homes. Not long after, Riis's dollhouse-like study, with its teakwood walls and handsome fireplace, also fell to the bulldozer.

But many years before, in 1949, occurred two events that fittingly memorialized the two essential aspects of Jacob Riis which have concerned me — photographer and citizen. One was a huge show at the Museum of Modern Art called "The Exact Instant," for which Edward Steichen assembled more than 300 photographs covering camera reporting for the past century. The list of 180 photographers included many celebrities. Most of them were represented by one or two prints; Jacob Riis had six. The publicity release for the show mentioned only four names and said of Riis's work, "a camera crusade never surpassed." Never before had there been space for Riis in a group photographic show; indeed, the museum previously had refused to buy his original prints. Now here he was holding his own among the five-star generals of photography. I watched large groups of people absorbed in his pictures. I was thrilled — for he was my "protégé." Later when I asked Roger William Riis if he had seen the show, he replied, "Yes, you bet, I got the notice of the Modern Arters and realized that all this springs out of the Alland pioneering."

The second event that year went beyond the parochial concerns of photography as an art and honored Riis the citizen. New York's Mayor William O'Dwyer proclaimed Jacob A. Riis Week in honor of the man who "gave to New York and to all America a newer and wider sense of civic conscience and responsibility." A dinner commemorating Riis's one hundredth birthday was held at the Waldorf Astoria. Inviting me to serve on the sponsoring committee Roger William Riis wrote: ". . . there will be many glittering stuffed shirts on the Committee, that is why we want an occasional unstuffed shirt." Speakers representing every segment of New York's peoples praised the citizenship of Jacob Riis, which had brought the city better housing, parks and playgrounds. I too felt honored, for Riis's photography was mentioned from the rostrum. Many years have passed since that night when I sat and listened to the speakers ring out the words of Jacob Riis. Today his words and his pictures speak to us with a power undiminished by the passing years. They speak, as Riis himself put it, with the power of fact — "the mightiest lever of this or of any day."

Jacob A. Riis:

the instantaneous camera and the consecrated pen

"Reporter Office at 301 Mulberry Street"

. . . Jacob A. Riis went to the New York *Tribune* (1877–88) and later to the *Evening Sun* (1888–99), as a police reporter . . . His activities at police headquarters led Riis to his life's work and the cleansing of the New York slums.

Dictionary of American Biography

51

"Dens of Death"

When the "Dens of Death" were in Baxter Street, big
barracks crowded out the old shanties. More came every day,
I remember the story of those shown in the picture.
They had been built only a little while when complaints came to
the Board of Health of smells in the houses. A sanitary
inspector was sent to find the cause. He followed the smell
down in the cellar, and digging there discovered that
the water pipe was a blind. It had simply been run into
the ground and was not connected with the sewer.

The Battle with the Slum

Hell's Kitchen and Sebastopol

Once, when I was taking pictures about Hell's Kitchen,
I was confronted by a wild-looking man with a club, who required
me to subscribe to a general condemnation of reporters as
"hardly fit to be flayed alive," before he would let me go,
the which I did with a right good will . . . What with one thing
and another, and in spite of all obstacles, I got my pictures,
and put some of them to practical use at once.

The Making of an American

An Open Trench, Potter's Field

I hired a professional photographer whom I found in dire straits . . .
he repaid me by trying to sell my photographs behind my back . . .
There was at last but one way out of it; namely, for me to get a camera
myself. This I did, and with a dozen plates, took myself
up the Sound to the Potter's Field on its desert island to make my
first observations . . . And I wanted a picture of the open trench.
I got it, too. In the sunlight of a January day on the
white snow I exposed that extra-quick instantaneous plate first for
six seconds, then for twelve, to make sure I got the picture . . .
it was so dark, almost black from over-exposure as to be almost
hopeless. The very blackness of my picture proved later on, when I
came to use it with a magic lantern, the taking feature of it.
It added a gloom to the show more realistic than any the utmost art
of professional skill might have attained.

The Making of an American

"A Boarder at the Rutgers Street Dump"

A reporter of "The Evening Sun" (Jacob A. Riis) penetrated
into the inner recesses of that Rutgers Street dump and renewed
an acquaintance with its occupants . . . They were there, entrenched
in their old quarters more firmly than ever, living, sleeping,
and carrying on their household even to the extent of a piggery—an
animal one, that is to say—adjoining their door.

Article, *Evening Sun,* March 18, 1892

Mulberry Street Police Station

Waiting for the Lodging to Open

61

"Police Station Lodgers"
Women's Lodging Room in the West 47th Street Station

. . . There are an even score of police stations in the city
that harbor lodgers today. Of these four admit only women, five men
only, and eleven both sexes. Some are worse than others;
a few only are now underground, the majority in the back yards over
the prisons and heated from these, receiving also the stenches
from the cells with their drunken occupants to add to their own foul
horrors. They have all been denounced from year to year . . .
But they are there unchanged, as if never a word had been said . . .

Article, Jacob A. Riis, New York *Tribune*, January 31, 1892

Eldridge Street Police Station Lodgers

"Elizabeth Street Police Station—Women Lodgers"

. . . The Elizabeth Street Station is one of the newer pattern
and accorded one of the best. Certainly the doorman seems to make
an effort to clean it out, but broom and hose do not prevail
against such an Augean stable as the tramp lodgers leave behind.
Elizabeth Street is close to the Mulberry Street Bend
and receives the overflow of its stale beer dives nightly. The
Health Inspector . . . last week figured that its cubic air space
allowed ten men and ten women lodgers . . . The returns from the precinct
for December last show that the men's room alone sheltered
in that month 548 lodgers. On December 5 the number that slept
in the space big enough for ten men was forty-eight . . .

Interview with Jacob A. Riis, *The World*, February 12, 1893

Same As Previous Page
Detail

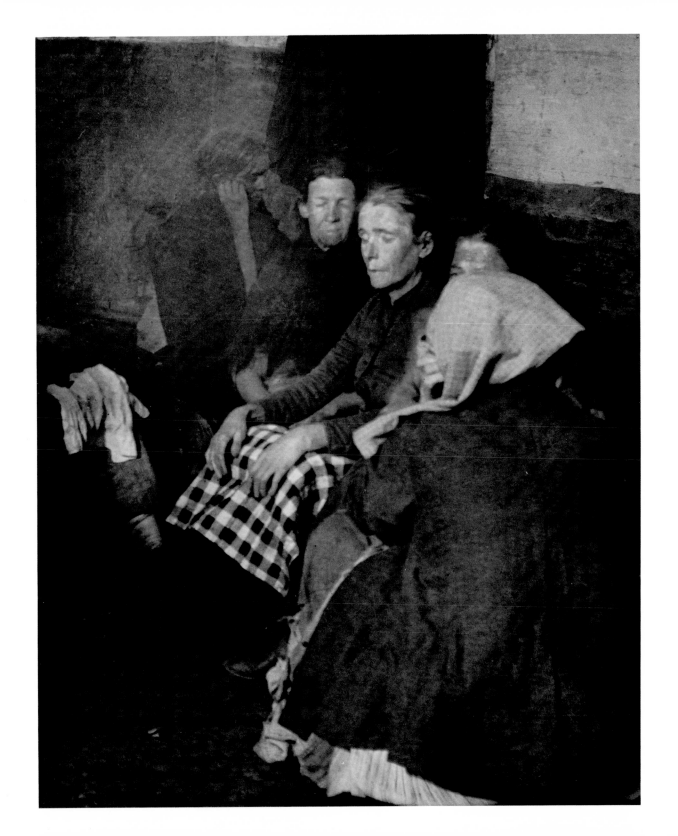

An Ancient Woman Lodger in Eldridge Street Police Station.
A "Scrub" with Her Bed

In 1889, 2,633 persons were charged with "vagrancy," 947 of
them women. A goodly proportion of these latter came from the low
groggeries of the Tenth Ward, where a peculiar variety of the
female tramp-beggar is at home, the "Scrub." The scrub is one degree
perhaps above the average pauper in this, that she is willing
to work at least one day in the week, generally the Jewish Sabbath.
The orthodox Jew can do no work of any sort from Friday
evening till sunset on Saturday, and this interim the scrub fills out . . .
The pittance she receives for this vicarious sacrifice of
herself upon the altar of the ancient faith buys her rum for at least
two days of the week at one of the neighborhood "Morgues" . . .

How the Other Half Lives

Police Station Lodging House

A gas jet burning dimly revealed four naked board walls.
In one corner a sink, in the other an open closet. A narrow
strip of the floor visible just inside the door, all the
rest hidden from sight by a double row of pine planks laid on
iron racks knee high from the floor, with a slight slant
from the wall. On each plank a human form lay stretched out or
curled up, asleep . . . That they were human shapes was
made certain by the snore they emitted. But for that, they might
have been at a casual glance taken for just so many piles of filthy
rags. The air was heavy with stenches unutterably disgusting.

Article, Jacob A. Riis, New York *Tribune*, January 31, 1892

Police Lodging Rooms, Church Street Station, in Which Jacob A. Riis Slept in 1870

. . . In the midnight hour we walked into the Church Street police station and asked for lodging . . . The lodging-room was jammed with a foul and stewing crowd of tramps. A loud-mouthed German was holding forth about the war in Europe (Franco-Prussian), and crowding me on my plank . . . Cold and hunger had not sufficed to put out the patriotic spark within me . . . and I told him what I thought of him and his crew . . . I smothered my disgust at the place as well as I could, and slept, wearied nearly to death . . .

Twenty-five Years Later

. . . Down the cellar steps to the men's lodging-room I led the President of the Police Board (Theodore Roosevelt). It was unchanged— just as it was the day I slept there. Three men lay stretched full length on the dirty planks . . . Standing there I told Mr. Roosevelt my own story. He turned alternately red and white with anger . . . Orders were issued to close the doors of the police lodging rooms on February 15, 1896 . . . The battle was won . . .

The Making of an American

Police Station Lodger

The typhus lodger in Eldridge Street police station. He lay
by the stove in the policemen's room, no one dreaming what ailed
him. Typhus is a filth disease, of all the most dreaded . . .
I warned them that there would be trouble with the lodging-rooms,
and within eleven months the prophecy came true. The typhus broke
out there. The night after the news had come I took my camera
and flash-light and made the round of the dens, photographing them all
with their crowds. Of the negatives I had lantern-slides made
and with these under my arm knocked at the doors of the Academy of
Medicine, demanding to be let in. They let me in, and that
night's doing gave the cause of decency a big push.

The Making of an American

"Happy Jack's Canvas Palace—A Seven-cent Lodging House"
Pell Street

. . . The twenty-five cent lodging house keeps up the pretence of
a bedroom . . . The fifteen-cent bed stands boldly forth without
a screen in a room full of bunks . . . At the ten-cent level the locker
for the sleeper's clothes disappears . . . A strip of canvas, strung
between rough timbers, without covering of any kind, does for the
couch of the seven-cent lodger . . . uneasy sleepers roll off at
intervals, but they have not far to fall to the next tier of bunks . . .
The proprietor of one of these seven-cent lodging houses was known to
me as a man of reputed wealth and respectability. He "ran" three
such establishments, and made . . . $8,000 a year clear profit . . . there
are no licensed lodging-houses known to me which charge less than
seven cents . . . though there are unlicensed ones enough where
one may sleep on the floor for five cents a spot, or squat in a sheltered
hallway for three. The police station lodging house, where the soft
side of a plank is the regulation couch, is next in order . . .

How the Other Half Lives

"Five Cents a Spot"
Unauthorized Lodgings in a Bayard Street Tenement

. . . What squalor and degradation inhabit these dens the health
officers know . . . From midnight until far into the small hours of
the morning the policeman's thundering rap on closed doors is heard . . .
The doors are opened unwillingly enough . . . upon such scenes as the
one presented in the picture. It was photographed by flashlight
on just such a visit. In a room not thirteen feet either way slept
twelve men and women, two or three in bunks set in a sort of alcove,
the rest on the floor. A kerosene lamp burned dimly in the fearful
atmosphere . . . The "apartment" was one of three in two adjoining
buildings we had found, within half an hour similarly crowded. Most
of the men were lodgers, who slept there for five cents a spot . . .

How the Other Half Lives

"Men's Lodging Room in the West 47th Street Station"

. . . Last year they [the police lodging houses] furnished
altogether 147,637 lodgings, and nearly twice as many during the
winter months, when there was no chance of ventilation as in
the summer. On a certain cold night last week . . . 577 homeless men
and women slept in them. On that night [there were] 12
men and 11 women in West 47th Street . . . [there] ballot booths
and other trappings of election business crowded the men's
lodging-room . . . A dozen shabby men snored among the lumber
wherever they could find room, flat on the wooden floor, with their
feet toward the stove. As many women sat or lay about in
the room across the hall . . .

Article, Jacob A. Riis, New York *Tribune*, January 31, 1892

"Night in Gotham Court"

. . . We will begin at the beginning . . . A hundred years ago, yes,
less than that, seventy-five years ago, there was no such thing as
a tenement house in New York City. It is a modern invention of the devil.
Here we are at the "cradle" of the tenement [Gotham Court] . . .
that alley has a bad record. A murder was committed there less
than a week ago, and it was not the first by a great many. In point of
nationality it is typical of all down-town of New York City. When
I took a census once of that alley, there were one hundred and forty families,
one hundred Irish, thirty-eight Italians, and two German, and not a
native born individual in the entire alley except the children . . .

. . . When the cholera came along some years ago, the ratio of deaths
was not over sixteen or seventeen to the thousand in the "clean"
wards up-town, but down there in that alley it was one hundred and
ninety-five to the thousand. That is what such a place stands
for in times of epidemic . . .

Illustrated lecture, Jacob A. Riis, 1894

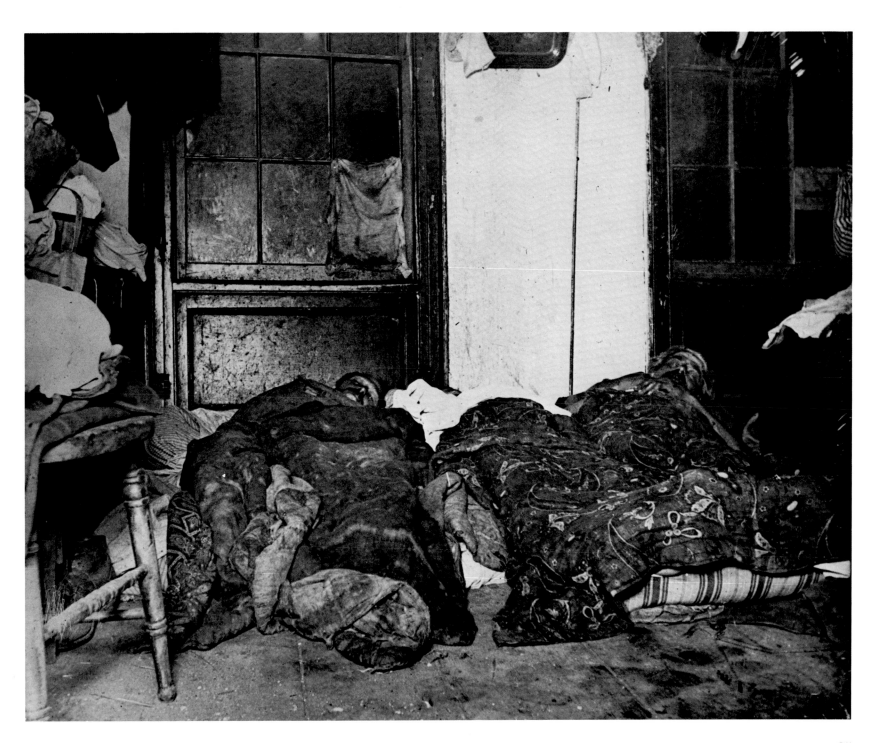

A Downtown "Morgue"

All the evil the saloon does in breeding poverty and
in corrupting politics; all the suffering it brings into the
lives of its thousands of innocent victims, the wives and
children of drunkards it sends forth to curse the community;
its fostering of crime and its shielding of criminals—
it is all as nothing to this, its offense . . . secret dives are
skulking in the slums and out of them . . . No one knows
the number of unlicensed saloons in the city . . .

How the Other Half Lives

Hell on Earth

One night, when I went through one of the worst dives
I ever knew, my camera caught and held this scene
that I set before you. When I look upon that unhappy girl's
face, I think that the Grace of God can reach that
"lost woman" in her sins; but what about the man who made
profit on the slum that gave her up to the street?

The Peril and the Preservation of the Home

A Black-and-Tan Dive in "Africa"

The moral turpitude of Thompson Street has been notorious
for years . . . The borderland where the white and the black races
meet in common debauch, the aptly-named black-and-tan-saloon,
has never been debatable ground from a moral stand-point.
It has always been the worst of the desperately bad . . . Usually it is
some foul cellar dive, perhaps run by the political "leader"
of the district, who is "in with" the police . . .

How the Other Half Lives

An All-Night Two-Cent Restaurant, in "The Bend"

... the stale-beer dive, is known about "the bend" by the
more dignified name of the two-cent restaurant. Usually, as in
this instance, it is in some cellar giving on a back alley.
Doctored, unlicensed beer is its chief ware. Sometimes a cup of
"coffee" and a stale roll may be had for the two cents. The men pay
the score. To the women—unutterable horror of the suggestion—
the place is free. The beer is collected from the kegs put
on the sidewalk by the saloon-keeper to await the brewer's cart,
and is touched up with some drugs to put a froth on it. The
privilege to sit all night on a chair, or sleep on a table, or
in a barrel, goes with each round of drinks.

How the Other Half Lives

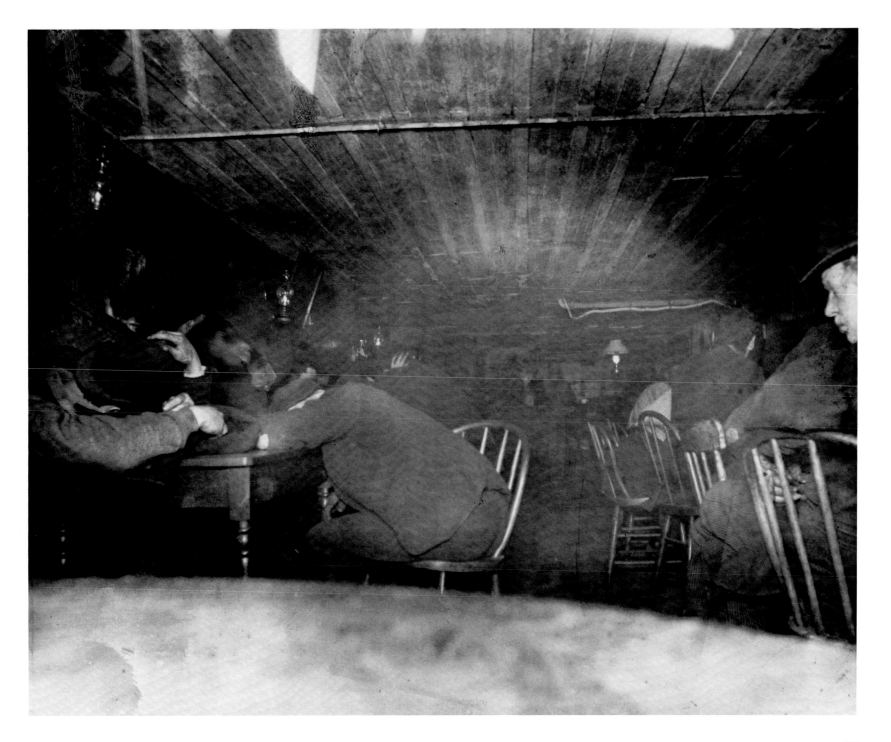

Battle Alley, Whyo Gang's Headquarters

This picture was evidence at a murder trial. The X marks
the place where the murderer stood when he shot his victim on
the stairs . . . In fifteen years I never knew a week to
pass without a murder there . . . it was the wickedest, as it
was the foulest, spot in all the city . . . The old houses
fairly reeked with outrage and violence. When they were torn down,
I counted seventeen deeds of blood in that place
which I myself remembered . . . The district attorney connected
more than a score of murders of his own recollection with
Battle Alley, the Whyo Gang's headquarters.

The Battle with the Slum

"Bandits' Roost"
59 ½ Mulberry Street

. . . At 59 Mulberry Street, in the famous Bend, is another alley
of this sort [like Baxter Street Alley] except it is as much worse in
character as its name, "Bandits' Roost," is worse than the designations
of most of these alleys. It has borne this name these many years,
and though there have been many entire changes in the occupants in that
time, each succeeding batch seems to be calculated in appearance
and character to keep up the appropriateness of that name . . . Many Italians
live here . . . They are devoted to the stale beer in room after room,
where the stuff is sold for two or three cents a quart.
After buying a round the customer is entitled to a seat on the floor,
otherwise known as a "lodging," for the night . . .

Article, New York *Sun*, February 12, 1888,
describing Jacob A. Riis's early flashlight photographs

"Mullen's Alley, Cherry Hill"

Among the pictures in Mr. Riis's collection are many
scenes described in the columns of the "The Journal" in connection
with the tenement-house crusade. One of these is known as "Mullen
Alley," located at No. 32 Cherry Street. It is seven feet wide at
the entrance, but narrows as you proceed, until at the other end
there is less than two feet of space between the walls . . . twenty-five
or thirty families most of them having many children, live in each
of the two houses between which it lies. Two wretched rooms, with
one window for each room, form the home of every family.

New York *Morning Journal,* February 12, 1888

"Baxter Street Alley,
Directly in the Rear of Bandits' Roost"

. . . At 59 Baxter Street . . . is an alley leading in from
the sidewalk, with tenements on either side crowding so close
as to almost shut out the light of day. On one side they
are brick and on the other wood, but there is little difference
in their ricketiness and squalor. This is . . . an Italian
colony, and the bags of rags and bones and paper shown
are gathered by these people, despite the laws and ordinances
and the 3,000 police . . .

Article, New York *Sun,* February 12, 1888,
describing Jacob A. Riis's early flashlight photographs

100

"Baxter Street Alley in Mulberry Bend"
(Now Destroyed)

. . . A handful of Methodist women made the Five Points decent.
To understand what that meant, look at the "Dens of Death" on Baxter
Street, which were part of it, "houses," said the Health
Inspector (1869), "into which the sunlight never enters . . . that are
dark, damp and dismal throughout all the days of the year,
and for which it is no exaggeration to say that the money paid to the
owners as rent is literally the 'price of blood.' " It took us
twenty-fours years after that to register the conviction in the form
of law that that was good cause for the destruction of a tenement
in cold blood; but we got rid of some at that time in a fit of anger.
The mortality officially registered in those "dens of death"
was 17.5 percent of their population . . .

The Battle with the Slum

"Nibsy's Alley at 47 ½ Crosby Street
Torn Down in the Fall of 1895"

(The hero of Jacob A. Riis's story *Nibsy's Christmas* is the
Giuseppe of *The Children of the Poor*)

. . . It was the death of little Giuseppe that brought me to his home,
a dismal den in a rear tenement down a dark and forbidding alley.
I have seldom seen a worse place . . . From this hole Giuseppe had
come to the [Mott Street Industrial] school a mass of rags, but with
that jovial gleam in his brown eyes that made him an instant favorite . . .
Giuseppe . . . was sent to an Elizabeth Street tenement for a little
absentee . . . "This girl is very poor," he said, presenting her to the
teacher, with a pitying look . . . [He] fished his only penny out of his
pocket—his capital for the afternoon's trade [as a newsboy]. "I
would like to give her that," he said. After that he brought her
pennies regularly . . . and took many a thrashing for it. He undertook
a general supervision of the child's education . . . Giuseppe was twelve
years old . . . There came an evening when business had been . . . so bad
he thought a bed on the street healthier for him than the Crosby Street
Alley. With three other lads in similar straights he crawled into the
iron chute that ventilated the basement of the post office . . .
and snuggled down on the grating. They were all asleep, when
fire broke out in the cellar. The three climbed out, but Giuseppe,
whose feet were wrapped in a mail-bag, was too late . . .

"Arch Under First Rear Tenement at 55 Baxter Street Leading to the Second Rear, with Stairs Up Which Vincenzo Nino Went to Murder His Wife in 1895"

. . . I counted back nineteen murders in the one block (in the Mulberry Bend area) . . . The last of them all is yet fresh in the public mind. It was the killing by Vincenzo Nino, the barber, of his hard-working, long-suffering wife, in the rear house at 55 Baxter Street, where a sort of tunnel led through an arch under the middle tenement to the rear. He killed her in the sight of her helpless children . . . For once in its career the Bend took a moral stand. It rose in sudden fury against the wife murderer, and beat down the door behind which he cowered, just as the police came, in time to save his miserable life . . . The house was deserted . . . The Bend knew it was haunted. To the day they tore it down the broken panel and the splash of blood remained . . .

Article, Jacob A. Riis, "The Clearing of Mulberry Bend,"
The Review of Reviews, August, 1895

"Shooting Craps: The Game of the Street"
Bootblacks and Newsboys

The mania for gambling is all but universal. Every street
child is a born gambler; he has nothing to lose and all
to win. He begins by "shooting craps" in the street and ends by
"chicking dice" in the saloon, two names for the same thing, sure to
lead to the same goal. By the time he has acquired individual
standing in the saloon, his long apprenticeship has left little
or nothing for him to learn of the bad it has to teach . . .

The Children of the Poor

Tenement Yard

I counted the other day the little ones, up to ten years
or so, in a Bayard Street tenement that for a yard has
a triangular space in the center with sides fourteen or fifteen
feet long, just enough for a row of ill-smelling
closets at the base of the triangle and a hydrant at the
apex. There was about as much light in this "yard"
as in the average cellar . . . I had counted one hundred and
twenty-eight in forty families.

How the Other Half Lives

"It Costs a Dollar a Month to Sleep in These Sheds"
Jersey Street

. . . In that yard were habitations (now gone) built of old boards
and discarded roof tin, in which lived men, women and children
that had been crowded out of the tenements. The rent collector did not
miss them, however. They paid regularly for their piggeries.
I feel almost like apologizing to the pig; no pig would have been
content to live in such a place without a loud outcry . . .

The Peril and the Preservation of the Home

The Tramp

On one of my visits to "the Bend" I came across a
particularly ragged and disreputable tramp, who sat smoking
his pipe on the rung of a ladder with such evident
philosophic contentment in the busy labor of a score of
ragpickers all about him, that I bade him sit for a picture,
offering him ten cents for the job. He accepted my
offer with hardly a nod, and sat patiently watching me from
his perch until I got ready for work. Then he took
the pipe out of his mouth and put it in his pocket, calmly
declaring that it was not included in the contract,
and that it was worth a quarter to have it go
in the picture ...I had to give in.

How the Other Half Lives

"Scene on the Roof of the Mott Street Barracks"

. . . There is a block of tenements, known as the Mott Street
Barracks . . . There are five buildings—that is five front and four rear
houses, the latter a story higher than those on the street . . .
There were 360 tenants . . . when the police census was taken in 1888,
and 40 of them babies . . . When the health officers got through with the
Barracks in time for the police census of 1891, the 360 tenants
had been whittled down to 238 . . . Persistent effort had succeeded in
establishing a standard of cleanliness . . . but still . . . the slum
remained and will remain as long as that rear tenement stands. In the
four years fifty-one funerals had gone out from the Barracks. The
white hearse alone had made thirty-five trips . . .

The Children of the Poor

. . . It is in hot weather, when life indoors is well-nigh unbearable
with cooking, sleeping, and working, all crowded into the
small rooms together, that the tenement expands . . . Then a strange and
picturesque life moves upon the flat roofs. In the day and early
evening mothers air their babies there . . .

How the Other Half Lives

"The 'Ship' in Hamilton Street"

. . . the queer old building . . . is "The Ship," famous for fifty years
as a ramshackle tenement filled with the oddest crowd. No one knows
why it is called "The Ship," though there is a tradition that
once the river came clear up here to Hamilton Street . . . More likely it
is because it is as bewildering inside as a crazy old ship, with
its ups and downs of ladders parading as stairs, and its unexpected
pitfalls. But Hamilton Street . . . is not what it was . . . a sailors'
mission has lately made its appearance . . . There are no dives there,
nothing worse than the ubiquitous saloon and tough tenements . . .

How the Other Half Lives

Tenement Baby

I went up the dark stairs in one of those tenements and
there I trod upon a baby. It is the regular means of introduction
to a tenement house baby in the old dark houses, but I never
was able to get used to it. I went off and got my camera and
photographed that baby standing with its back against the public
sink in a pool of filth that overflowed on the floor.
I do not marvel much at the showing of the Gilder Tenement House
Committee that one in five of the children in the rear
tenement into which the sunlight never comes was killed by the
house. It seemed strange, rather, that any survived.

The Peril and the Preservation of the Home

The Trench in the Potter's Field

In the common trench of the Poor Burying Ground they lie
packed three stories deep, shoulder to shoulder, crowded in death
as they were in life, to "save space"; for even on that desert
island the ground is not for the exclusive possession of those
who cannot afford to pay for it.

How the Other Half Lives

A Flat in the Paupers' Barracks
with All Its Furniture

In Poverty Gap, an English Coal-Heaver's Home

Suspicions of murder . . . brought me to this house, a
ramshackle tenement on the tail-end of a lot over near the North
River docks. The family in the picture lived where the dead
woman lay . . . A patched and shaky stairway led up to their one bare
and miserable room, in comparison with which a whitewashed
prison-cell seemed a real palace. A heap of old rags,
in which the baby slept serenely, served as the common sleeping-
bunk of father, mother, and children . . .

How the Other Half Lives

"Home of an Italian Ragpicker"
Jersey Street

. . . Sometimes they ask me, What is all this about, with your
"infant slaughter" in the tenements? The children are bright and strong to
look at . . . A doctor once . . . said, "It is a clear case of the survival
of the fittest. Only those who are strong as cattle can ever stand it."
Those who are sick or dying you do not see . . . Come with me . . .
when those stony streets are like fiery furnaces, and see those mothers
walking up and down the pavements with their little babes . . . and hear
the feeble wails of those little ones! . . . Here is one of them, an Italian
baby in its swaddling clothes. You have seen how they wrap them
around and around until you can almost stand them on either end, and they
won't bend, so tightly are they bound. It is only a year ago that the
Italian missionary down there wrote to the city mission that he did not know
what to do with these Italian children in the hot summer days,
for "no one asked for them." They have been asked for since, thank God!

Illustrated lecture, Jacob A. Riis, 1894

"One of Four Pedlars Who Slept in the Cellar
of 11 Ludlow Street Rear"

. . . It was only last winter [1891] I had occasion to visit
repeatedly a double tenement at the lower end of Ludlow Street, which
the police census showed to contain 297 tenants, 45 of whom were
under five years of age, not counting 3 pedlars who slept in the mouldy
cellar, where the water was ankle deep on the mud floor.
The feeblest ray of daylight never found its way down here . . . It was an
awful place, and by the light of my candle the three, with their
unkempt beards and hair and sallow faces, looked more like hideous ghosts
than living men. Yet they had slept here among and upon decaying
fruit and wreckage of all sorts . . . for over three years . . . There had been
four. One was then in the hospital . . . He had been run over in
the street . . . Upstairs, especially in the rear tenement, I found the
scene from the cellar repeated with variations . . .

The Children of the Poor

"Ready for Sabbath Eve in a Coal Cellar"
A Cobbler in Ludlow Street

These cellars! . . . They [the tenants] are buried,
literally, alive . . . This hole is their "home," their all . . . The
Board of Health has ordered the family out . . . But it will
require the steady vigilance of the police for many months to
make sure that the cellar is not again used for a living-room.
Then it will in all probability be turned into a coal-cellar or a
shoe-shop by a cobbler of old boots, and the Sanitary Police in
their midnight tours will find it a bedroom for mayhap
a dozen lodgers, all of whom "happed in," as the tenant
will swear the next day, and fell asleep there . . .

Article, Jacob A. Riis, *Journal*, December 22, 1895

"Shoemaker Working in a House in the Yard of
219 Broome Street, Which the Landlord Built When the Sanitary Police
Put Him Out of the Basement. Clatterpole Sticks Up Through His House.
Rent $12 a Month."

. . . Rome had its walls, as New York has its rivers, and they
played a like part in penning up the crowds . . .That is the first chapter of
the story of the tenements everywhere . . . Step now across eighteen
centuries and all the chapters of the dreary story . . . and look upon this
picture of the New World's metropolis as it was drawn in public
reports at a time when a legislative committee came to New York to
see how crime and drunkenness came to be the natural crop of a population
"housed in crazy old buildings, crowded, filthy tenements in
rear yards, dark, damp basements, leaking garrets, shops, outhouses and
stables converted into dwellings, though scarcely fit to shelter
brutes," or in towering tenements . . .

The Battle with the Slum

"In Sleeping Quarters—Rivington Street Dump"

... The effort of no less than three departments of the City
Government, the Street Cleaning, the Health and the Fire
Department, were enlisted in ousting the dump dwellers after
an investigation that sent a shudder through the town . . .
[However] they were there, entrenched in their old quarters
more firmly than ever, living, sleeping, and carrying on their
`household . . . There are sixteen of them [dumps] . . . In every
instance the old conditions, that were held to be dangerous to
the city's health and property, have been reproduced in aggravated
form. Gangs of Italians who work on the scows live under the dumps.
It is their only home . . . Filth is their stock-in-trade, their environment,
their atmosphere, all there is of life to them . . .

Article, Jacob A. Riis, *Evening Sun*, March 18, 1892

"Under the Dump at West 47th Street"

. . . I made a personal inspection of the dumps along both
rivers last winter [1891] and found the Italian crews at work there
making their home . . . among the refuse they picked from the
scows. The dumps are wooden bridges raised above the level of the
piers upon which they are built to allow the discharge of the
carts directly into the scows moored under them. Under each bridge,
a cabin had been built of old boards, oil-cloth, and the like,
that had found its way on the carts . . . And here, flanked by
mountains of refuse, slept the crews of from half a dozen to three times
that number of men, secure from the police, who had grown
tired of driving them from dump to dump . . . There were women at some
of them, and at four dumps . . . I found boys who ought to have been
at school, picking bones and sorting rags . . . It was their home.
They were children of the dump, literally . . .

The Children of the Poor

"Minding the Baby"
Cherry Hill

. . . Of Susie's hundred little companions in the alley
—playmates they could scarcely be called—some made artificial
flowers, some paper-boxes, while the boys earned money at
"shinin'" or selling newspapers. The smaller girls "minded the baby,"
so leaving mother free to work . . . In an evening school class
of nineteen boys and nine girls . . . I found twelve boys who "shined,"
five who sold papers, one of thirteen years, who by day was
the devil in a printing-office and one of twelve who worked in a
wood-yard. Of the girls, one was thirteen and worked
in a paper-box factory, two of twelve made paper lanterns, one
twelve-year-old girl sewed coats in a sweat-shop, and one of the same age
minded a push-cart every day. The four smallest girls were
ten years old, and of them one worked for a sweater .. The three
others minded the baby at home; one of them found time to help her
mother sew coats when baby slept . . .

The Children of the Poor

"I Scrubs"
—Katie, Who Keeps House in West Forty-ninth Street

"What kind of work do you do?" I asked. "I scrubs," she
replied promptly, and her look guaranteed that what she scrubbed
came out clean. Katie was one of the little mothers whose
work never ends. Very early the cross of her sex had been laid upon
the little shoulders that bore it so stoutly. On the top
floor of a tenement . . . she was keeping house for her older sister
and two brothers, all of whom worked. Katie did the cleaning
and the cooking of the plain kind. She scrubbed and swept and went to
school all as a matter of course and ran the house generally with
an occasional lift from the neighbors, who were poorer than they . . .

The Children of the Poor

"Street Arabs in Sleeping Quarters"

. . . The Street Arab is as much of an institution in New York
as Newspaper Row, to which he gravitates naturally . . . Crowded out of
the tenements to shift for himself . . . he meets there a host of adventurous
runaways from every state in the Union . . . A census of the
population in the newsboys' lodging-house . . . will show such an odd mixture
of small humanity as could hardly be got together in any other spot.
The Street Arab has all the faults and all the virtues
of the lawless life he leads . . . Anyone, whom business or curiosity has
taken through Park Row or across Printing House Square in the
midnight hour, when the air is filled with the roar of great presses . . .
has seen little groups of these boys hanging about the newspaper
offices: in winter . . . fighting for warm spots around the grated vent-holes
that let out the heat and steam from the underground press-rooms
. . . and in summer playing craps and 7-11 on the curb for their hard-earned
pennies . . . Here the agent of the Society for the Prevention of
Cruelty to Children finds those he thinks too young for "business"
but does not always capture them . . .

How the Other Half Lives

The Street Arab has all the faults and all the
virtues of the lawless life he leads. Vagabond that he is,
acknowledging no authority and owing no allegiance
to anybody or anything, with his giving fist raised against
Society whenever it tries to coerce him, he is as bright
and sharp as the weasel . . . His sturdy independence, love of
freedom and absolute self-reliance, together with his
rude sense of Justice that enables him to govern his
little community, is not always in accordance with Municipal
Law or City Ordinances . . .

How the Other Half Lives

A Growler Gang in Session

While I was getting the camera ready, I threw out a vague
suggestion of cigarette-pictures, and it took root at once. Nothing
would do then but that I must take the boldest spirits of the
company "in character." One of them tumbled over against a shed,
as if asleep, while two of the others bent over him searching
his pockets with a deftness that was highly suggestive. This they
explained for my benefit, was to show how they "did the trick."

How the Other Half Lives

"What the Boys Learn on Their Street Playground"

... It [the street] taught him gambling as its first lesson,
and stealing as the next ... From shooting craps behind the "cops" back
to filching from the grocer's stock or plundering a defenceless
pedlar is only a step. There is in both the spice of law-breaking that
appeals to the shallow ambition of the street as heroic. At the
very time when the adventurous spirit is growing in the boy, and his games
are all of daring, of chasing and being chased, the policeman
looms up to take a hand, and is hailed with joyful awe. Occasionally,
the raids have a comic tinge. A German grocer wandered into
police headquarters with an appeal for protection against the boys. "Vat
means dot 'cheese it'?" he asked, rubbing his bald head in helpless
bewilderment. "Efery dime dey says 'cheese it,' somedings was gone."

The Battle with the Slum

Blind Beggar

. . . Nothing short of making street begging a crime has availed
to clear our city of this pest to an appreciable extent . . .
The blind beggar alone is winked at in New York's streets, because the
authorities do not know what else to do with him . . . The annual
pittance of thirty or forty dollars which he received from the City
serves to keep his landlord in a good humor; for the rest his
misfortune and his thin disguise of selling pencils on the street
corners must provide. Until the City affords him some systematic
way of earning his living by work . . . to banish him from the street would
be tantamount to sentencing him to death by starvation. So
he possesses it in peace, that is, if he is blind in good earnest . . .

How the Other Half Lives

"The Mongomery Guards"
(A Growler Gang)

I came once upon a gang of young rascals passing the growler
after a successful raid . . . and having my camera along,
offered to "take" them. They were not old and wary enough to be
shy of the photographer . . . or their vanity overcame
their caution. It is entirely in keeping with the tough's character
that he should love of all things to pose before a
photographer, and the ambition is usually the stronger the more
repulsive the tough.

How the Other Half Lives

"The Short Tail Gang (Corlears Hook)
Under the Pier at the Foot of Jackson Street
(Now Corlears Hook Park)"

. . . It is a bad picture, but it is not nearly so bad as
the place. Dock rats, those, drinking beer under a dump. That
is their business by day, drinking beer, loafing around,
seeing what they can pick up. At night they come out and
sneak along the water front . . . It happens every day especially in
the summer time, that a body floats ashore with the pockets
turned inside out . . . These [gangsters] are the fellows that
start out with the idea that the world owes them a living, and
that they are going to collect it as easily as they can . . .

Illustrated lecture, Jacob A. Riis, 1894

"Hunting River Thieves—Dock Rats Pursued by the Police at Night"

. . . By day they [the gangs of New York] loaf in the corner-groggeries on their beat, at night they plunder the stores along the avenues, or lie in wait at the river for unsteady feet straying their way . . . The tipsy wayfarer is their chosen victim . . . Should he foolishly resist or make an outcry—dead men tell no tales . . . Police patrol the rivers as well as the shore on constant look-out for them [the dock-rats], but seldom catch up with them. If overtaken after a race during which shots are often exchanged from the boats, the thieves have an easy way of escaping and at the same time destroying the evidence against them; they simply upset the boat. They swim, one and all, like real rats; the lost plunder can be recovered at leisure the next day by diving or grappling. The loss of the boat counts for little. Another is stolen, and the gang is ready for business again . . .

How the Other Half Lives

"The Verdict of the Rogues Gallery"

That such conditions as were all about us should result
in making "toughs" of the boys was not strange. Rather, it
would have been strange had anything else come of it.
With the home corrupted by the tenement; the school doors closed
against them where the swarms were densest, and the children
thrown upon the street, there to take their chance; with
honest play interdicted, every natural right of the child turned
into a means of oppression, a game of ball became a crime
for which children were thrust into Jail, indeed, shot down like
dangerous criminals when running away from the policeman;
with the lawlessness of the street added to want of rule at home . . .
it seemed as if we had set out to deliberately make trouble
under which we groaned.

The Making of an American

HIGHWAYMAN AT 17

BURGLAR AT 17

MURDERER AT 19

PICKPOCKET AT 15

HANGED AT THE TOMBS

BURGLAR AT 18

HIGHWAYMAN AT 18

PICKPOCKET AT 13

HIGHWAYMAN AT 18

163

"Knee-Pants" at Forty-five Cents a Dozen
—a Ludlow Street Sweater's Shop

Up the flights of dark stairs, three, four, with new smells
of cabbage, of onions, of frying fish, on every landing, whirling
sewing machines behind closed doors betraying what goes on within
to the door that opens to admit the bundle and the man. A sweater,
this, in a small way. Five men and a woman, two young girls,
not fifteen, and a boy . . . are at the machines sewing knickerbockers,
"Knee-pants." The floor is littered ankle-deep with half
sewn garments. The faces, hands, and arms to the elbows of everyone
in the room are black with the color of the cloth . . .

How the Other Half Lives

"Necktie Workshop in a Division Street Tenement"

. . . The bulk of the sweater's work is done in the tenements,
which the law that regulates factory labor does not reach . . . Ten
hours is the legal work-day in the factories, and nine
o'clock the closing hour at the latest. Forty-five minutes at
least must be allowed for dinner, and children under
sixteen must not be employed unless they can read and write English;
none at all under fourteen. The very fact that such a law
should stand on the statute book, shows how desperate is the plight
of these people. But the tenement has defeated its benevolent
purpose. In it the child works unchallenged from the
day he is old enough to pull a thread. There is no such thing
as a dinner hour; men and women eat while they work, and the
"day" is lengthened at both ends . . . far into the night . . .

How the Other Half Lives

"In a Sweat Shop"

("12 year old boy at work pulling threads. Had sworn
certificate he was 16—owned under cross-examination to being
12. His teeth corresponded with that age.")

. . . I have in my desk a table giving the ages at which children
get their teeth . . . I had been struggling with the problem of
child-labor in some East Side factories, and was not making any
headway. The children had certificates, one and all,
declaring them to be "fourteen," and therefore fit to be employed.
It was perfectly evident that they were not ten in scores of cases . . .
There seemed to be no way of proving the fact, yet the fact was
there and must be proven. My own children were teething at the time,
and it gave me an idea. I got Dr. Tracy to write out that table
for me . . . Armed with that I went into the factories and pried
open the little workers' mouths . . . Even allowing for the backwardness
of the slum, it was clear that a child that had not yet grown
its dog-teeth was not "fourteen," for they should have been out at
twelve at the latest. Three years later the Reinhardt Committee
reported to the legislature that the net result of the
factory law was a mass of perjury and child-labor, and day began to
dawn for the little ones, too . . .

The Making of an American

"Sewing Pants for the Sweater"
—in Gotham Court

... I saw women finishing "pants" at thirty cents a day.
Some of the garments were of good grade, and some of poor; some of
them were soldier's trousers, made for the government, but
whether they received five, seven, eight cents a pair, it came to
thirty cents a day ...

... Look at Gotham Court, described in the health reports of the
sixties as a "packing-box tenement of the hopeless back-to-back type"
... The stenches from the "horribly foul cellars" with their
"infernal system of sewerage" must needs poison the tenants all
the way up to the fifth story. I knew the court well, knew the gang
that made its headquarters with the rats in the cellar ...
knew the well-worn rut of the dead wagon and the ambulance to the
gate ... but I have lived to see it taken in hand three times. And a
good deal was accomplished ... Gotham Court [demolished c.1898] contained
142 families when I made a canvass of it in the old days, comprising
700 persons, not counting the vagrants who infested the cellars ...

The Battle with the Slum

"Little Susie at Her Work"
Gotham Court

Little Susie, whose picture I took while she was pasting
linen on tin covers for pocket flasks . . . is a type of
the tenement-house children whose work begins early and ends late.
Her shop is her home. Every morning she drags down to
her Cherry Street Court heavy bundles of the little tin boxes much
too heavy for her twelve years, and when she has finished
running errands and earning a few pennies that way, takes her
place at the bench and pastes two hundred before it is
time for evening school. Then she has earned sixty cents
—"More than Mother," she says with a smile . . .

The Children of the Poor

"Indians [Iroquois] at Broome Street"

. . . Within hail of the Sullivan-Street School, camps
a scattered little band. . . They are Indians, a handful of
Mohawks and Iroquois, whom some ill wind has blown down
from their Canadian Reservation, and left in these
west-side tenements to eke out such a living as they can
weaving mats and baskets, and threading glass pearls
on slippers and pincushions, until, one after another, they
have died off and gone to happier hunting-grounds . . .
There were as many families as one could count on the
fingers of both hands when I first came upon them . . .
Last Christmas there were seven . . .

Jacob A. Riis, "Merry Christmas in the Tenements,"
The Century, December, 1897

Sewing and Starving in an Attic

. . . The oldest, the mother, who had struggled along with
her daughter making cloaks at half a dollar apiece, twelve long
years since the daughter's husband was killed in a street
accident and the city took the children, made the bitter confession:
"We do get so kind o' downhearted living this way, but we
have to be where something is going on, or we just can't stand it."
There was sadder pathos to me in her words than in the
whole long story of their struggle with poverty; for
unconsciously she voiced the sufferings of thousands, misjudged
by a happier world, deemed vicious because they are
human and unfortunate.

How the Other Half Lives

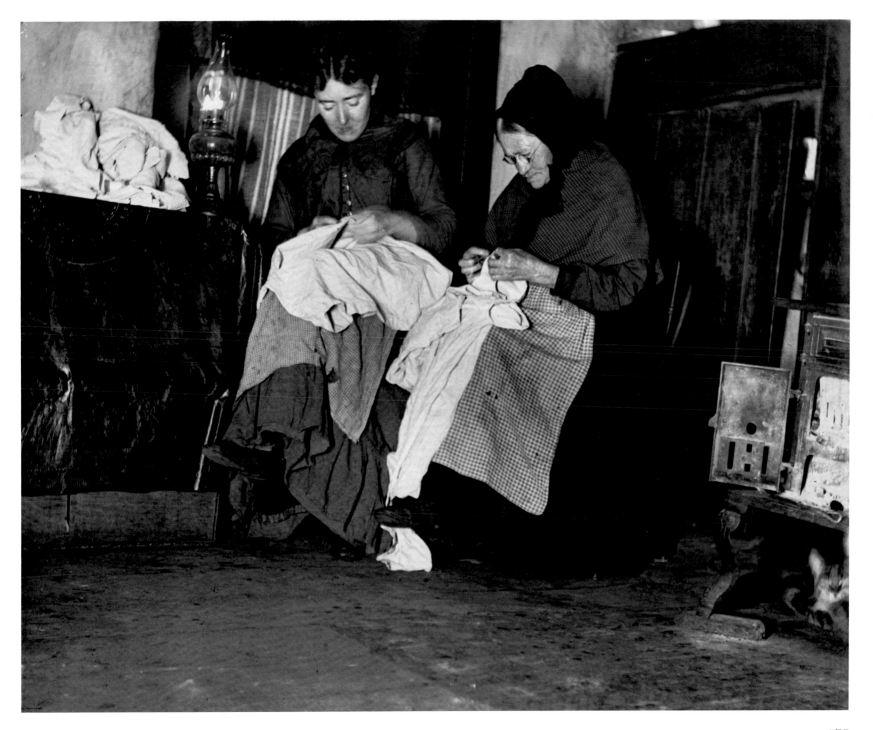

"Old Mrs. Benoit in Her Hudson Street Attic"

. . . I had about made up my mind that the only real Americans
[the Indians] in New York did not keep the holiday at all, when one
Christmas Eve, they showed me how. Just as dark was setting
in, old Mrs. Benoit came from her Hudson-Street attic—where she
was known among the neighbors, as old and poor as she, as
Mrs. Ben Wah, and believed to be the relict of a warrior of the name of
Benjamin Wah—to the office of the Charity Organization Society,
with a bundle for a friend who had helped her over a rough spot—
the rent, I suppose . . . [It] contained a lot of little garments
which she had made out of remnants of blankets and cloth of her own
from a younger and better day . . . "For those," she said . . .
"who are poorer than myself"; and hobbled away. I found out, a
few days later, when I took her picture weaving mats in her
attic room, that she had scarcely food in the house that Christmas
Day and not the car-fare to take her to church! . . . Mrs. Ben Wah . . .
is not really an Indian; but her husband was one . . .

Jacob A. Riis, "Merry Christmas in the Tenements,"
The Century, December 1897

"A Class in the Condemned Essex Market School, with the Gas Burning by Day"

. . . Indeed, the jail filled the title role in the educational
cast of that day. Its inmates were well lodged and cared
for, when the sanitary authorities twice condemned the Essex Market
school across the way as wholly unfit for children to be in, but
failed to catch the ear of the politician who ran things unhindered.
When [in 1894] I denounced the "system" of enforcing—or not
enforcing—the compulsory education law as a device to make thieves
out of our children by turning over their training to the street,
he protested angrily; but the experts of the tenement house commission
found the charge fully borne out of the facts . . . Five years we
strove with the powers of darkness, and look now at the change!
The New York School system is not yet the ideal one—it may never
be: but the jail, at least, has been cast out of the firm . . .

The Battle with the Slum

"East Side Public School"

. . . In New York we put boys in foul, dark class-rooms,
where they grow crooked for want of proper desks; we bid them play
in gloomy caverns which the sun never enters, forgetting that
boys must have a chance to play properly, or they will play
hookey; we turn them away by thousands from even such delights as
these, and in the same breath illogically threaten them with
the Jail if they do not come . . .

Jacob A. Riis, "The Making of Thieves in New York,"
The Century, November 1894

Talmud School in Hester Street

It is true that these tenement schools that absorb several
thousand children are not what they might be from a sanitary point
of view. It is also true that heretofore nothing but Hebrew
and the Talmud have been taught there. But . . . the wise and patriotic
men who are managing the Baron de Hirsch Charity are . . .
gathering the teachers in and setting them to learn English. Their
new knowledge will soon be reflected in their teaching and
the Hebrew Schools become primary classes in the system of public
education. The School in a Hester Street tenement . . . is a
fair specimen of its kind—by no means one of the worst—and so
is the back yard behind it, that serves as the children's
play-ground, with its dirty mud-puddle, its slop barrels, and its
foul tenement-house surroundings.

The Children of the Poor

"Night School in the Seventh Avenue Lodging House"
(Run by The Children's Aid Society)

. . . There is very little to hold the boy who has never known
anything but a home in the tenement . . . Left alone to himself, he soon
enough finds a place in the police books . . . but he is not left
alone . . . What the Society for the Prevention of Cruelty to children
is to the baby-waif, The Children's Aid Society is to the
homeless boy . . . The good it has done cannot easily be over-estimated. Its
lodging-houses, its schools and its homes block every avenue
of escape with their offer of shelter upon terms which the boy soon
accepts, as on the whole cheap and fair . . .

How the Other Half Lives

. . . One night I took the picture of my little vegetable
peddling friend, Edward, asleep on the front bench in evening school.
Edward was nine years old and an orphan, but hard at work every
day earning his own living by shouting from a peddler's cart. He could
not be made to sit for his picture, and I took him at a
disadvantage . . . I was anxious not to have the boy disturbed, so the
spelling-class went on while I set up the camera . . .

The Children of the Poor

"The First Patriotic Election
in The Beach Street Industrial School"

The Industrial School plants itself squarely in the gap
between the tenement and the public school . . . The Children's Aid Society
maintains twenty-one in seventeen of the City's twenty-four wards,
not counting twelve evening schools, five of which are in the
Society's lodging houses . . . The American Female Guardian Society
conducts twelve such day schools . . . the two Societies' schools last year
reached a total enrolment of nearly fifteen thousand children . . .
the school is distinctly Italian, Bohemian, Hebrew or mixed;
the German, Irish, and colored children coming in under this head, and
mingling usually without the least friction. Very lately a unique
exercise has been added to the course in these schools . . . It is called
"saluting the flag" . . . Then was evolved the plan of letting the
children decide for themselves whether or not they would so salute the flag
. . . while incidentally instructing them in the duties of the voter . . .
Ballot-boxes were set up in the schools on the day before the last election.
The children had been furnished with ballots . . . the week before,
and told to take them home to their parents, a very apt reminder
to those who were naturalized citizens of their own duties . . .
On Monday morning the children cast their votes . . . with all the solemnity
of a regular election . . . eighty-two percent of the whole number of
enrolled scholars turned out for the occasion, and of the 4,306 votes
cast, 88, not quite two percent, voted against the flag . . .

The Children of the Poor

"The Survival of the Unfittest"

I photographed that phase of the battle with the slum
before they shut in the last tenement in the block with a factory
building in its rear. It stood for a while after that down
in a deep sort of pocket with not enough light struggling down on
the brightest of days to make out anything clearly in the rooms
—truly a SURVIVAL of the unfittest; but the tenants stayed . . .
But at length business claimed the last foot of the block,
and peace came to it and to us.

The Battle with the Slum

The Walls Began to Give

Something that needed me in Mulberry Street had come. I was
in a death-grapple with my two enemies, the police lodging-room and
the Bend . . . The first guns that I have any record of were
fired in my newspaper in 1883 . . . the guns I speak of were not the
first that were fired—they were the first I fired . . .
When my fellow workers smiled, I used to remind them of the Israelites
that marched seven times around Jericho and blew their
horns before the walls fell. "Well, you go ahead and blow yours,"
they said; "You have the faith." And I did, and the walls
did fall, though it took nearly twice seven years. But they came down,
as the walls of ignorance and indifference must every time,
if you blow hard enough and long enough, with faith in your cause
and in your fellow-man. It is just a question of endurance.
If you keep it up, they can't.

The Making of an American

"Prayer-time in the Nursery
—Five Points House of Industry"

. . . The Five Points Mission and the Five Points House of
Industry have accomplished what no machinery of government availed
to do. Sixty thousand children have been rescued by them from
the streets . . . their work still goes on, increasing and gathering in the
waifs, instructing and feeding them, and helping their parents
with advice and more substantial aid . . . The House of Industry is an
enormous nursery-school with an average of more than four
hundred day scholars and constant boarders . . . It is one of the most
touching sights in the world to see a score of babies, rescued
from homes of brutality and desolation . . . saying their prayers in the
nursery at bedtime. Too often their white night-gowns hide
tortured little bodies and limbs cruelly bruised by inhuman hands.
In the shelter of this fold they are safe, and a happier little group
one may seek long and far in vain . . .

How the Other Half Lives

205

Poverty Gap-pers Playing Coney Island

... More than two-hundred children were digging, swinging, see-sawing, and cavorting about the Poverty Gap playground when I looked in on a hot Saturday afternoon ... Long files of eager girls, whose shrill voices used to make the echoes of the gap ring with angry clamor, awaited their turn at the scups, quiet as mice and without an ill word ... The street that used to swarm with mischievous imps was as quiet as a church ... The retiring toughs have dubbed it "Holy Terror Park" in memory of what it was, not of what it is.

The Children of the Poor

"Mulberry Bend"

. . . I had at last an ally (my photographic evidence)
in the fight with the Bend . . . From the day—I think it was
in the winter of 1886—when it was officially doomed
to go by act of legislature until it did go, nine years later,
I cannot remember that a cat stirred to urge it on . . .
By a sort of tacit consent, the whole matter was left to me as
the recognized Mulberry Bend crank . . . The Bend was a much
jollier adversary than the police lodging houses. It kicked back
. . . In the twenty years of my acquaintance with it as a
reporter I do not believe there was a week in which it was not
heard from in the police reports, generally in connection
with a crime of violence . . . So, between the vendetta, the Mafia,
the ordinary neighborhood feuds, and the Bend itself,
always picturesque, if outrageously dirty, it was not hard
to keep it in the foreground . . .

The Making of an American

Note: Mulberry Bend Park replaced Mulberry Bend.
It was the first park obtained as a result of the passage of the
Small Parks Act in 1887, and was formally opened on June 15, 1897.

The Mulberry Bend Became a Park

The Mulberry Bend we laid by the heels; that was the
worst pigsty of all, and here again let me hark back to the
murder I have spoken of so often. I do not believe that
there was a week in all the twenty years I had to do with the
den, as a police reporter, in which I was not called to
record there a stabbing or shooting affair, some act of violence.
It is now five years since the Bend became a park and the
police reporter has not had business there during that time; not
once has a shot been fired or a knife been drawn. That is
what it means to let the sunlight in!

The Peril and the Preservation of the Home

Winter at Richmond Hill in Front of Our House

The deeper I burrowed in the slum, the more my
thoughts turned, by a sort of defensive instinct, to the
country. My wife laughed and said I should have
thought of that while we yet had some money to buy or build
with but I borrowed no trouble on that score . . .
Edward Wells offered to lend me what more I needed to buy lots,
and the manager of our Press Bureau built me a house
and took a mortgage for all it cost. So before the next
winter's snows we were snug in the house . . . with a
ridge of wooded hills, the "backbone of Long Island," between
New York and us. The very lights of the city were shut out.
So was the slum, and I could sleep.

The Making of an American

Bibliography

Riis manuscript material is scattered
in many archives. Most important and numerous in:

1. The Library of Congress, Washington, D.C.
   Collection of letters, lectures, scrapbooks,
   clippings and pocket diaries, formerly in possession
   of Riis family: Mary Phillips Riis, Mrs. John Riis,
   Mr. Roger William Riis and Kathryn Riis Owre.
2. The New York Public Library.
   Original holograph MSS. of five books. Correspondence,
   1892–1914. Lecture notes, 1896, 1906, 1909, 1911.
   Clippings, pamphlets and other ephemera.
3. Dan America Archives, Aalborg, Denmark.
   Letters from Jacob Riis to his family: one dated
   1870; others, from 1894–1914 (almost all in Danish).
4. American Academy of Arts and Letters.
   Letters and material on reforms.

The Riis bibliography is enormous. A comprehensive
listing of newspaper stories and magazine articles is in
Louise Ware's book, *Jacob A. Riis: Police Reporter,
Reformer, Useful Citizen* (D. Appleton-Century Co., 1938).

The new edition of *The Making of an American* by Jacob A.
Riis with an Epilogue by J. Riis Owre gives much new
information on Riis's later life not obtainable before
(Macmillan Co., 1970).

Books by Jacob A. Riis

How the Other Half Lives (1890).
Children of the Poor (1892).
Nibsy's Christmas (1893).
Out of Mulberry Street (1898).
A Ten Years War (1900).
The Making of an American (1901).
The Battle with the Slum (1902).
Children of the Tenements (1903).
The Peril and Preservation of the Home (1903).
Is There a Santa Claus? (1904).
Theodore Roosevelt, the Citizen (1904).
The Old Town (1909).
Hero Tales of the Far North (1910).
Neighbors (1914).
Christmas Stories (anthology, 1923).

The Making of an American appeared in translation:
Comment Je Suis Devenu Américain
(Louis Michaud, Paris, 1908).
Hvordan Jeg blev Amerikaner
(Gyldendalske Boghandel Nordisk Forlag,
Copenhagen, 1912).
La Formación de un Americano
(Plaza & Janes, S. A., Buenos Aires, 1965).
Minha Historia Dorea
(Rio de Janeiro, 1964).

References

Page	Column	Line	
5	2	3	"the despair that lives ..." Circular letter, National Urban League, 1973.
8			Preface by Ansel Adams. *Photo-Notes,* 1947.
11	1	19	"The photograph is not the newest ..." *Photography and the American Scene,* 1938, p. 449.
12	1	7	"Stieglitz returning to New York in 1890 ..." *America and Alfred Stieglitz,* 1934, p. 76.
12	1	25	"Lewis Mumford has written of Stieglitz ..." *Ibid.,* p. 50.
13	1	7	"Society of Amateur Photographers ..." *Ibid.,* p. 81.
13	1	27	"The esthetic, selfless, sympathetic touch ..." *Ibid.,* p. 80.
13	1	37	"Group show at the Metropolitan Museum of Art ..." Six American Documentary Photographers, 1890–1915.
13	2	14	"Dr. P. H. Emerson, who said ..." *Encyclopaedia Britannica,* 14th edition.
13	2	21	"Edward was in seventh heaven ..." *U.S. Camera Annual,* 1940.
14	1	36	"Muckraking, Steffens once suggested ..." *Adventure in American Literature,* 1948, p. 238.
14	2	24	"In the words of Roy Stryker ..." *Creative Camera,* Jan. 1969.
14	2	34	"There was very little truly constructive imagery ..." Letter to the author, Dec. 1973.
15	1	6	"The theme is housing ..." An American Group, Rockefeller Center show, 1937.
15	1	19	"Art is one of the forms of Social ..." Stuart Davis, May 1936.
15	1	31	"The photographs appeared in the ..." *P.M.* weekly, July 21, 1940.
15	2	12	"There is no denying ..." James Baker Hall, *Afterimage,* Sept. 1973.
15	2	29	"His biographer, Dr. Louise Ware ..." Jacob A. Riis, *Police Reporter, Reformer, Useful Citizen,* 1938, p. 292.
16	1	11	"In a Methodist revival ..." *The Making of an American,* Macmillan, 1901, p. 134.
18	1	9	"There were 15 of us in the Latin School ..." Jacob Riis, *The Old Town,* Macmillan, 1909.
18	2	36	"Put him in a black skin ..." Louis Adamic, *A Nation of Nations,* 1944, p. 201.
19	1	4	"I have not forgotten my religion ..." Letter from Riis to his friends, May 4, 1870. Dan-America Archives, Aalborg, Denmark.
22	1	28	"this is the place; these narrow ways ..." *The Works of Charles Dickens,* P. F. Collier, Vol. V, p. 294.
22	2	13	"Forty thousand vagrants ..." *Sunshine & Shadow in New York,* 1868, p. 208.
25	1	35	"The rewards in journalism go to ..." *Public Opinion,* 1938, pp. 334, 340.

26   1   7   "One morning scanning my newspaper . . ."
The Making of an American, p. 267.

28   2   29   "held delapidated rookeries . . ."
Felix Riesenberg and Alexander Alland,
    Portrait of New York, Macmillan, 1939, p. 18.

30   2   8   "In fact, the first large scale use . . ."
Paper by James Peck, *Image,* Nov. 1955.

33   2   30   "Recently a man, well qualified . . ."
The Redemption of New York, Press Scrap Book,
    1902, p. 147.

34   1   8   "Permit me to say it . . ."
Jacob Riis, *The Peril and the Preservation of the
    Home,* 1903, p. 15.

34   2   3   "In sharp contrast to Riis's practical . . ."
"American Issues," *The Social Record,* 1944,
    Vol. I, p. 333.

34   2   16   "My own faith in racial brotherhood . . ."
Alexander Alland and James Waterman Wise,
    Viking Press, 1945.

38   1   10   "I was to lecture at Cedar Falls . . ."
A History of Our Time, Vol XVI, 1908,
    p. 10490.

40   2   9   "I've heard a little swearing . . ."
N.Y. *World Telegram,* May 27, 1947.

45   1   36   "the interrelation of the three . . ."
Beaumont Newhall, *The History of Photography,*
    1949, p. 166.

45   2   11   "I first heard about the trunks . . ."
Mr. Kennerley said he heard the story from
    Robert Lingel, Acquisition Div. of N.Y.P.L.

Index

About the Author

Alexander Alland was born in Sebastopol, Crimea. During the Civil War, after his graduation from an academy, he left Russia and went·to Turkey. During his three years' stay in Constantinople he worked as a photographer's assistant and later, at the age of nineteen, was put in charge of a portrait studio. In 1923, with the money received from the sale of his camera and equipment, he bought passage in steerage and, as a ward of the League of Nations, sailed to America. He arrived in New York without a cent.

After years of work at various jobs, he went back to his first choice and became a free-lance photographer. Gradually, fascinated by our polyglot population, he involved himself in taking pictures of the life, work and folklore of our many ethnic groups. He was the first photographer to make extensive studies of Gypsies, Black Jews, Chinese, New York City American Indians, and others. His photo-essays appeared in numerous newspapers and magazines, and in books dealing with the problems which our different national, racial and religious groups face in living and working together.

During the depression of the 1930's Mr. Alland super-vised the Photo-Mural Section of the Federal Art Project and taught advanced photography in the American Artists School. Later he was employed as instructor in the photography workshop of the National Youth Administration. He participated in numerous group exhibitions and was given one-man shows in the New School for Social Research and the Museum of the City of New York. His work is included in the collections of the Museum of Modern Art, the New York Historical Society, the New York Public Library, the Schomberg Collection and the Museum of the City of New York.

During the Second World War the Office of War Information, U.S. Department of State, as well as various church, civic and educational organizations, drew heavily on his files dealing with minority groups. He served as photo editor of *Common Ground*, a publication of the Common Council for American Unity, and director, Pictures for Democracy, Council Against Intolerance in America, and was a member of the American Artists Congress.

His books *American Counterpoint* and *The Springfield Plan* were each chosen as one of the Fifty Best Books of the Year.